Southern Living

ideas for great
BEDROOMS

This sophisticated scheme hints of the West Indies with an upholstered sleigh bed, wall-to-wall seagrass on the floor, and flowing linen draperies.

Oxmoor House®

DECORATIVE ARTIST: N. E. LARKIN

A flea-market find gains a colorful new life.

Sweet Dreams

Flexible, hardworking, and fun—today's bedrooms reflect our growing need for efficient yet stylish private retreats. This book provides plenty of fuel for daydreams, then follows up with practical pointers that can help you turn ideas into action.

More than 130 inspiring photos form the book's core; you'll find a colorful gallery of possibilities in "Great Bedrooms," pages 25–67. If it's the nuts and bolts you need, turn to "A Shopper's Guide," pages 69–95. And for the beginning designer, "A Planning Primer," pages 7–23, provides a sequential course in space planning and decorating.

We thank the many design professionals and homeowners who shared ideas with us and allowed us to photograph their installations. We also thank Antique Accessories, Carpet Center, City Lights, Michael Duté Fine Art Interiors, and Floorcraft for accessories used in our photographs.

Cover design by James Boone and Vasken Guiragossian. Photography by Cheryl Sales Dalton, Southern Progress Photo Collection.

Southern Living® Ideas for Great Bedrooms was adapted from a book by the same title published by Sunset Books.

Book Editor
Scott Atkinson

Coordinating Editor
Linda J. Selden

Consulting Editor
Jane Horn

Editorial Coordinator
Vicki Weathers

Copy Editor
Marcia Williamson

Design
Joe di Chiarro

Illustrations
Susan Jaekel

Photo Styling
JoAnn Masaoka Van Atta

Computer Production
Linda Bouchard

Our appreciation to the staff of *Southern Living* magazine for their contributions to this book.

First printing January 2000
Copyright © 2000 by Oxmoor House, Inc.
Book Division of Southern Progress Corporation
P.O. Box 2463
Birmingham, Alabama 35201
Southern Living® is a federally registered trademark of Southern Living, Inc.

ISBN 0-376-09074-X
Library of Congress Catalog Card Number: 99-65014
Printed in the United States

CONTENTS

SPECIAL FEATURES

RISE AND SHINE

Get ready for a wake-up call, because today's bedrooms are much more than a rumpled bed and a chest of drawers.

Whether you're planning to revamp a master bedroom, a tiny guest room, a chaotic kids' space, or a detached in-law suite, current options in layout, decor, and furnishings are sure to inspire you.

Today's layouts are flexible. Though the style may range from traditional prints to polished steel, the bedroom has evolved into a modern, multiuse space—while still serving its original role as a private refuge. Master bedrooms now harbor home offices, sunny window seats, home theaters, even art collections.

Master-suite schemes can create self-sufficient retreats and buffer zones, often integrating bath, walk-in closet, dressing area, his-and-her vanities, and makeup center into one seamless whole. And what about adding an overstuffed chair and a

DESIGN: JACOBSON, SILVERSTEIN & WINSLOW ARCHITECTS/PAUL WINANS CONSTRUCTION INC.

A young boy's room is in a league of its own

A cedar-and-granite dressing area

fireplace, an exercise alcove, or a private whirlpool and sauna?

If space is at a premium, hard-working storage built-ins can make the most of it. Look to the sleeping area for possibilities: platform beds, storage beds, lofts, pullouts, futons, and updated Murphy beds all gain you floor space.

And has anyone ever had enough closet space? You'll find both sophisticated modular cabinets and freestanding, one-of-a-kind wardrobes and armoires. Racks, bins, pullouts, drawers, hooks, and other accessories are abundant. Now it's easy to put everything in its place (though *keeping* it there is another matter).

Today's bedroom can be a place for work. Whether you're telecommuting or simply scrolling through the household budget, computers, CPUs, printers, fax machines, and home copiers create new design challenges. Who wants to stare at all that clutter? Fortunately, built-ins and other options can tame it.

And, of course, a bedroom is for relaxing. Surround-sound and home-theater units are showing up in lots of master bedrooms, suites, and multiuse guest rooms. You might add a coffee bar, sink, hot-water dispenser, and under-counter refrigerator—or even a popcorn machine.

There's also new emphasis on light and openings—walls of ganged windows, skylights, roof vaults. French and sliding doors can double as windows while leading the way to a sunny pocket deck or patio.

Why not grab a snack, fluff up the pillows, and adjust your reading light? Perhaps the bedroom of your dreams is but a few pages away.

Country-elegant iron bed and plaid fabrics

A sun-splashed bedside tub

DESIGN: J. REED ROBBINS

A PLANNING PRIMER

W hether it's a luxurious master wing, a hardworking guest room, or simply a new color scheme you want to achieve, your project's success depends on good planning. This chapter can serve as a workbook for getting organized.

Think of bedroom design as a three-step process. First, survey what you already have and analyze your options for improving it. Next, think about how to lay out space and use the components of your room the way they'll work best for you. Finally, consider the style, colors, and decorative touches that will pull together the look you want.

For inspiration and ideas, look through the photos in the chapter "Great Bedrooms" (pages 25–67). For shopping tips and information on beds, fabrics, light fixtures, and other materials, see pages 69–95.

The contrasting colors in this master bedroom exude a quiet elegance. The ceiling's cool blue combines with the yellow of the walls to bathe the room in soft light. The contemporary iron canopy bed is on a grand scale to complement the room's high ceilings.

GETTING STARTED

First things first. Before you plunge headfirst into a bedroom shopping spree, take time to assess what you have now. Begin by identifying your general needs and options, then render your present floor plan onto paper, with detailed observations about it.

WHAT ARE YOUR OPTIONS?

If you're planning a new home or an addition, you may have the luxury of choosing the ideal size and location for your new bedroom. Perhaps it's time for that spacious master suite, complete with study, window seat, and soothing spa. Or maybe you need to create a buffer zone between your repose and a teenager's amplified heavy-metal explorations. If you're starting from scratch, the options are open.

Most of us, however, are limited by space and layout restrictions where we currently live. Even so, you may have more choices than you think. A simple face-lift can work amazing changes. A new window bay, a walk-in closet, or a lifted ceiling can make a surprisingly dramatic difference. Or maybe an attic conversion can provide the quiet you've been looking for. You'll find examples of all these approaches, and many more, in the photos throughout this book.

Updating existing space. One of the easiest and most instantly gratifying improvements you can make is updating. Replacing old wallpaper, adding recessed downlights, and rolling out a cushy carpet, for example, can give a tired bedroom a bright, fresh look.

Though it won't solve underlying problems with the basic floor plan or boost available space, this type of remodel is the easiest for a do-it-yourselfer and will often do as much for a dreary room as rearranging the walls—at half the cost.

Six Remodeling Strategies

Updating surfaces

Crown and base moldings

Windows

Wallpaper

Reclaiming unused space

Converting basement

Redefining space

Removing partition wall

Removing ceiling and exposing beams

Redefining space. In contrast to a simple update, reassigning interior space allows you to alter your home's floor plan to make the space you already have more usable and efficient.

Taking down a wall or opening up a ceiling can bring in light and contribute a new feeling of spaciousness. Conversely, adding a wall to divide a large space can give you two separate bedrooms (or a sleeping area and a study) instead of one. Individual spaces for sleeping and desk work needn't be huge; perhaps two people can share an existing closet area or bath. Adding a wall is usually a simple proposition; taking one out may not be (see "Structural Concerns" on page 11).

Another way to stretch space is to add a bay window or dormer. Such a unit can replace an existing window or be installed where no opening existed before. A cantilevered popout can provide several feet of new floor space—without the expense of a new foundation.

Room conversions. If an interior redesign won't solve your problem, try looking up, down, and around. It's possible that at least some of the space you need already exists and can be converted to a new use. The three most obvious choices are the attic, basement, and garage.

An attic room should allow a minimum of 7½ feet ceiling height over at least half of the floor area. What is often considered a liability—the sloping walls—can become an asset with creative planning. Insulation and ventilation can help tame summer heat; dormer and/or roof windows help spread natural light.

Hillside homes often have substantial crawl spaces beneath the floor, perhaps reaching minimum ceiling height as the grade falls away. Basement rooms can be "clammy," it's true, but with good insulation and a garden exposure you may be able to make the space quite snug and dry.

A garage may present a great opportunity, provided you can solve the logistics of routing utilities to this location. But remember, if you cut into your garage space, you may be required to provide off-street parking somewhere else.

Adding on. You can go up, down, or sideways—add a second story or basement, build on a one- or two-story addition, or extend the front, back, or side of the house.

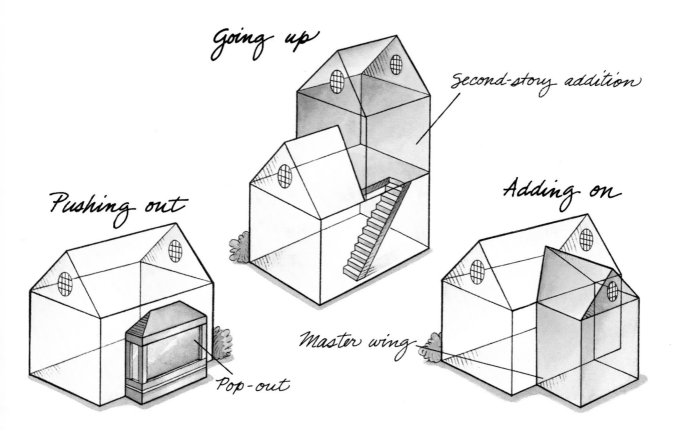

Going up

Second-story addition

Pushing out

Adding on

Pop-out

Master wing

Adding a second floor is probably the most challenging way to remodel your house. Compared to reshaping existing space or expanding a house laterally, adding a second story can be a demanding, expensive, and intrusive operation. But if your house already fills your lot, if you want to preserve garden space, or if you yearn for views that reach beyond your neighbor's rooftop, adding a second story might be worth the trouble.

Since blending a new floor with an existing house presents both structural and aesthetic challenges, you'll probably need the help of an architect and a structural engineer. Together they must determine whether the existing foundation can bear the weight of the added floor; where to position supporting pads, posts, and stiffening shear walls; and how to tie the new roof into the old. Other concerns are where to locate stairways and whether the addition should rise abruptly from the foundation or step back to make the house seem less massive.

Adding laterally may be the best way to expand your house when you have a generous lot. But tacking on an extra room won't necessarily make your home more comfortable. How will the new space be used? Will its function be compatible with the function of adjacent spaces? Can you extend or expand a circulation pattern—for instance, by linking a new bedroom with an existing hallway or reworking existing spaces to create an efficient, comfortable connection?

TAKING STOCK

A clear, accurate base map—like the one shown below—can be one of your most effective planning tools. It also helps you communicate with design professionals and showroom personnel.

Measure the space. First, sketch out your present layout (don't worry about scale), doodling in windows, doors, closets, and other features. Then, using a folding wooden rule or a steel tape, measure each wall, plus the sizes and locations of any openings or irregularities.

Here's an example, using a hypothetical bedroom: beginning at one corner, measure the distance to the outside of the window frame, from there to the opposite edge of the window frame, from this edge to a built-in cabinet, and so on to the opposite corner. After you finish one wall, total the figures; then take an overall measurement

A Sample Base Map

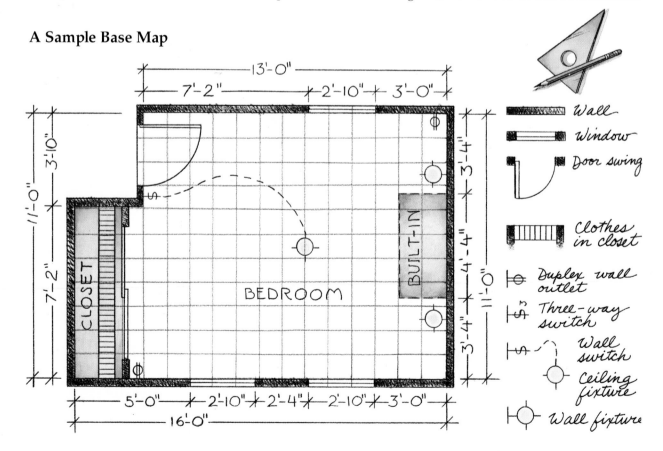

from corner to corner. The two figures should match. Measure the height of the wall in the same manner.

Do the opposite walls agree? If not, something's out of whack; find out what it is. Also check all corners with a carpenter's square or by the 3-4-5 method: measure 3 feet out from the corner in one direction, and 4 feet in the other direction, then connect the points with a straightedge. If the distance is 5 feet, the corner is square.

Make a base map. Now draw your bedroom to scale on graph paper. Most designers use ½-inch scale (¼4 actual size). An architect's scale is helpful though not essential, but using a T-square and triangle and some good drafting paper with a ¼-inch grid will make the job a lot easier.

If you own a personal computer, you may wish to try one of the many design programs currently available. The latest offerings are considerably more user-friendly and much less costly than earlier CAD programs aimed at professionals.

The sample plan shown at left includes dimension lines and electrical symbols—outlets, switches, and fixtures. Be sure to indicate door swings, windows, skylights, and any heating ducts or returns. It's also helpful to note the direction of joists (see drawing at right), mark any bearing walls, and sketch in other features that might affect your remodeling plans. And if you're considering "borrowing" space from an adjacent room or hallway, add its features to your map as well.

Record your thoughts. A wish list can help organize your responses to your present bedroom. Over the course of a week, jot down thoughts and impressions directly onto one or more copies of your base map. Don't worry about consistency, and don't worry about cost at this point; you can always cut back later.

What do you like about your present space? What do you dislike? Do you want more morning light? Is storage lacking? To help stimulate your responses, look through the pictures in "Great Bedrooms" (pages 25–67), and browse through some design magazines.

Sum up your concerns on a separate sheet of paper, adding any important preferences or dislikes that you discover. Then gather up your list, any clippings you've collected, and a copy of your base map, and get ready to start brainstorming.

STRUCTURAL CONCERNS

I f you're planning to open up a cramped space, install a skylight, or add a master-suite spa, your bedroom remodel may require some structural modifications. Here's a crash course.

As shown below, walls are either *bearing* (supporting the weight of ceiling joists and/or second-story walls) or *nonbearing*. If you're removing all or part of a bearing wall, you must bridge the gap with a sturdy beam or posts. Nonbearing (also called *partition*) walls can usually be removed without too much trouble—unless pipes or wires run through them. You can also add a wall or divider with few structural challenges. You may have to beef up joists in the attic floor so it can support the "live" weight of foot traffic—not just the ceiling below it.

Doors and windows need special framing, as shown. Skylights require similar openings in ceiling joists and/or rafters. A skylight may also need a light shaft to direct light from the roof to a ceiling opening.

Any remodel must maintain not only structural integrity but the style of both your house and neighborhood as well. If you have questions, it's best to call in an architect or structural engineer for advice.

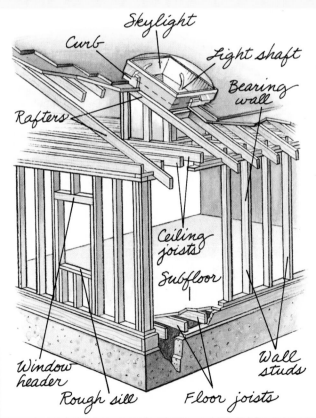

EXPERIMENTING WITH YOUR IDEAS

Once you've surveyed the general scope of your project, begin to block out the space. Here's where your base map comes in handy. To experiment with your ideas, place tracing paper over your map and sketch on top, or make photocopies of the map and draw directly on them. Make cutouts representing your furniture (use the same scale as for the room itself) and move them around on the map until you find the spot that works best for each piece; for examples, see page 14.

Bed Clearance Guidelines

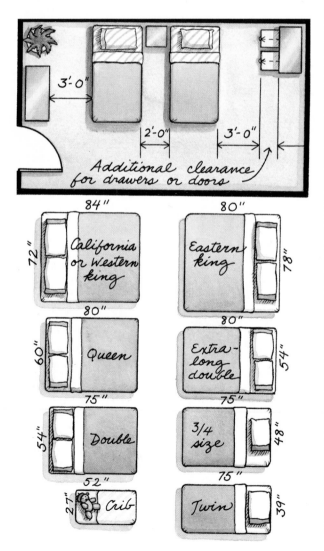

BEGIN WITH THE BED

Since most of the time spent in the bedroom is spent in or on the bed, it should be treated as the room design's starting point. For example, the view *from* the bed may be more important than the view *of* the bed. Traffic patterns begin and end at the bed, and the location of satellite areas, such as a dressing table or sitting area, will evolve from the bed's placement.

In the chapter "A Shopper's Guide" (pages 69–95), we discuss bed types from A to W—from adjustable beds to water beds. Beds can be freestanding, positioned with one end or side against a wall, angled into the room, or tucked into a corner or a special niche. If you need to make the most of limited floor space or if the room you're designing is for occasional guests, a loft bed, bunk bed, Murphy bed, trundle, or other built-in may be the answer.

Opinions vary on how much space is necessary around a bed, but 3 feet between the bed and a wall or other vertical surface seems generous. Two feet between a bed and another low surface—such as another bed—allows minimum room to stand and make the bed. Where a door swings inward or drawers pull out, be sure to allow extra clearance. Especially with a platform bed, clearance above the bed is important. Four feet of headroom is the minimum for sitting upright.

Trace the outline of your bed atop the base map in the place you think works best. Then try drawing lines for the paths you'll take from one part of the room to another. What will your morning pattern be? How can you avoid retracing your steps? Without putting obstacles in your path, how can you make the most of seemingly wasted floor space? What's the most direct route to the bathroom? Where will you sit when you put on your shoes?

Try to imagine yourself in the room. From the bed, what will you see? Will morning light waken you gently, or glare into your eyes? Will there be drafts? Will you be able to reach a light switch? Where will you put a book and your glasses? What's the ceiling like? Will an overhead fixture shine in your eyes? Try out rough solutions on a copy of your map.

Closet Planning at a Glance

THINK STORAGE

Whether you're adding a new bedroom or redesigning an existing one, you'll want to give some careful thought to clothes storage. Your first decision is between built-in and freestanding pieces; pages 76–80 run down some good choices.

Next, evaluate your closet capacity. Most closets are either the roomy, walk-in type or the shallow but lengthy wall type. Both have their advantages. In general, people with large wardrobes prefer the walk-in closet, simply because it holds more. But with good space planning and double-decker closet rods, a wall closet can often accommodate the same amount of clothing.

Shelves, drawers, pull-out bins, and racks can make either closet more efficient. Several manufacturers offer modular closet systems.

Before you purchase any storage aids or design a new closet, take careful stock of what you need to store. Start by eliminating clothing that you don't—or won't—wear. Then sort your clothing into categories and take some measurements. Find out just how much room you need to store your shoes, or the height at which dresses should be hung so their hems won't drag on the floor. Then you'll be able to determine if your present closet—with the addition of another rack or two—will give you sufficient space.

Knowing the general dimensions of items in the basic clothing categories can help you plan just how much room to allow for each article. The drawing above gives measurements based on standards established by the American Institute of Architects.

Bedroom Component Cutouts

½ inch equals 1 foot

18" x 78" Dresser
21" x 38" Armoire
30" x 30" Chair
18" x 60" Dresser
20" x 48" Chest
24" Night table
21" x 21" Chair
21" x 21" Chair
19" x 39" Chest
12" Lamp
12" Lamp
12" x 60" Bookcase
32" x 60" Loveseat
22" x 24" Rocking chair
24" x 26" Chair
24" x 26" Chair
25" x 50" Desk
18" x 24" Table
18" x 24" Table
24" x 24" Night table
14" x 16" Chair
14" x 16" Chair
18" Plant stand
36" x 90" Chaise longue
12" x 48" Bookcase

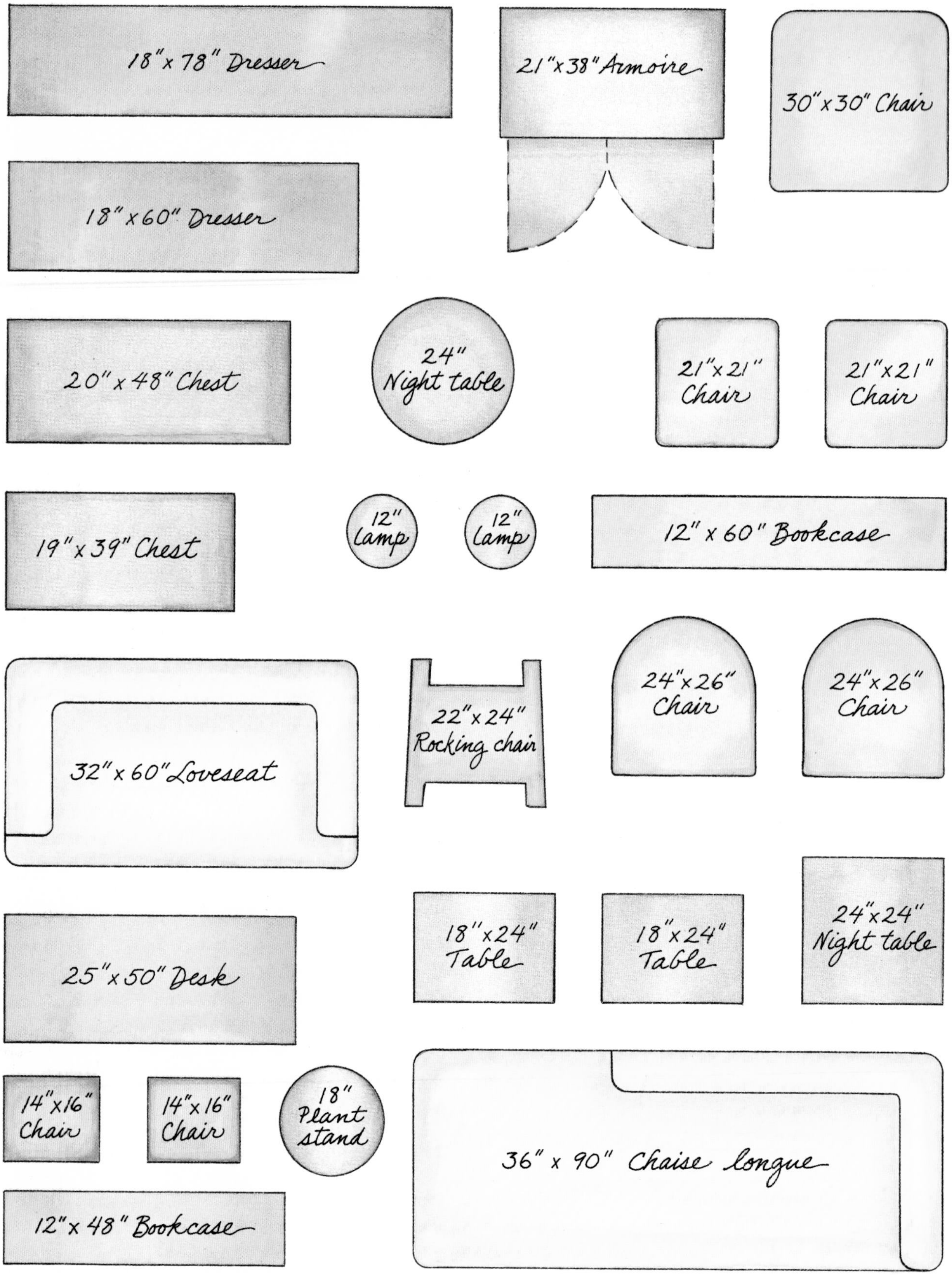

If necessary, consider ways to enlarge your present closet, or think about where you can build a new one. Using space occupied by an adjacent hallway can help take pressure off the bedroom closet.

DRESSING AREA?

If you'd like a traditional dressing table, now's the time to sketch it on your plan. Where will you store cosmetics, jewelry, and accessories? What mirrors and lighting (see pages 92–95) will you need?

A walk-in closet can neatly combine clothes storage with a dressing area. About 3 feet of clear space between rows of hanging garments allows ample room to dress. You should allow a minimum depth of about 1½ feet for each row of hangers; 2 feet is preferable.

If space permits, this area can serve as a bridge between bedroom and bath. Good ventilation, especially for a closet adjacent to a shower or tub, can be crucial.

SITTING AREA?

Just moving a comfortable chair into the bedroom turns the room into a sitting area as well as a sleeping space. Built-in seating economizes on space; traditional options include banquettes or window seats.

A sitting room that's right *off* the bedroom rather than right *in* it has the advantage of letting you close a door between the two areas, reserving the bed chamber itself for sleeping. On the other hand, the main purpose of the sitting area might be to allow interaction through the whole room.

OFFICE OR WORK SPACE?

Your work area can be a room next to the bedroom, a space shared with the sleeping quarters, or even a structure connected to the bed.

A study or studio next to the bedroom, separated by a door, has two virtues—association with a bedroom's privacy, plus all the advantages of a separate room. Sliding doors or bifolds allow you to unite the spaces when you choose.

An extra closet—an already built-in alcove—is a natural spot to convert to a tiny bedroom office.

Using it won't rob the bedroom of floor space, though it may create a shortage of clothes storage.

Some people like to work on, or even in, the bed. If you're one of them, make it convenient by installing work surfaces, communications such as a telephone and intercom, and good lighting.

NOISE & PRIVACY

Be sure to acknowledge your needs for both privacy and quiet in the bedroom. Privacy can be ensured by window treatments (see pages 88–89) or, if the room fronts a street or outdoor living area, by bringing in light through glass block, skylights, or high clerestory windows.

To baffle household noise, you might consider soundproofing the walls and/or ceiling (see page 82). To soften the impact of sound within the room, choose thick carpeting, fabric wall coverings, or an acoustic ceiling.

HEATING & VENTILATION

Check to see if the new bedroom will be adequately served by your present heating system. If not, you'll need to reroute ductwork to the area or add an auxiliary room heater. An auxiliary heater may offer the advantage of energy efficiency. With a separate control, even a timer, you can heat the room only when you need to.

In warm climates, be sure the placement of windows allows for cross-ventilation. An openable skylight can help dispel hot air; a ceiling fan promotes air movement.

BARRIER-FREE BASICS

If you are remodeling to accommodate a disabled or elderly person, be aware of this person's special needs. Minimum heights, clearances, and room dimensions may be required. The door should swing out to allow easy movement in and out of the room. You may also want to install grab bars, use levers in place of knobs, and choose furniture and accessories specifically designed for the disabled.

A barrier-free bedroom needn't look like a hospital room. An architect or designer in your area may specialize in this field; it's worthwhile to check out the latest options.

Orienting Windows & Skylights

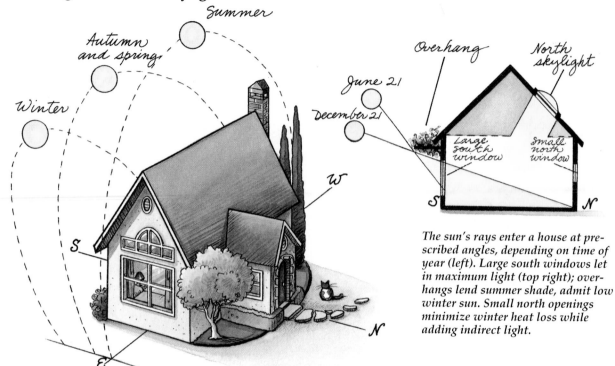

The sun's rays enter a house at prescribed angles, depending on time of year (left). Large south windows let in maximum light (top right); overhangs lend summer shade, admit low winter sun. Small north openings minimize winter heat loss while adding indirect light.

ADDING AMENITIES

Now is also the time to work any amenities into the mix; you'll find plenty of inspiring options throughout this book. Are you considering a coffee bar in the dressing area? Dreaming of a wall system for a bedroom media center? A private fitness center? A library? An under-counter refrigerator?

Bedside phones have become standard in many homes. To keep in touch, you may want to build in an intercom to other rooms or a control panel for your security system (see pages 94–95). Many homeowners are adding bedside switches for all main interior and exterior lights.

What about other master-suite additions, such as a fireplace, whirlpool tub, or auxiliary vanity and sink? Sketch the possibilities onto fresh copies of your base map.

DOORS, WINDOWS & SKYLIGHTS

Doors, windows, and skylights—often lumped together as "openings"—have a great deal to do with how your bedroom relates to the spaces around it.

The best door for a bedroom is a solid one, not a noise-transmitting, hollow-core type. A door located near a corner will interfere with furniture less than one in the middle of a wall. Adding a hinge-stop to a door will allow you to place furniture behind it. Remember to install a wall switch on the nonhinged side of each door.

Interior doors needn't be impenetrable barriers. Single- or multipane panels of glass admit light while sealing off noise and drafts; choose frosted or diffused glass to protect privacy. Pocket doors are great space savers.

The placement, size, shape, and number of windows will have a significant effect on the amount of light they bring into a room. A south-facing window (north-facing in the southern hemisphere) will let in the most light and is desirable in all but hot climates. A window oriented to the north provides soft, diffuse light. Do you want cheery east light to wake you in the morning, or are you a night owl who prefers a more subdued way to rise?

The sun also travels from north to south and back again over the course of each year (see drawing above). Permanent or seasonally mounted exterior awnings, canopies, and overhangs are effective for keeping summer sun out while maximizing precious winter warmth and light. Other options include exterior shutters or shades and interior window coverings.

A skylight adds light, a view, and in some cases ventilation without affecting privacy or taking up any wall space. For soft, uniform light, use a north-facing skylight or one with either translucent glazing or a diffusing panel at the ceiling level. You'll need to build a light shaft if there's an attic or crawl space between the roof and ceiling (see drawing on page 11).

A general rule of thumb for determining skylight size is to allow 1 square foot of skylight area for every 20 square feet of floor space. Additional glazing can open up a small room but may squander energy. The deeper your light shaft and the higher your ceiling, the larger your skylight will have to be to provide the desired amount of light.

NIGHT LIGHTING

Once the sun goes down, lighting becomes necessary: ambient lighting so you can see the other end of the room; task lighting for reading; and perhaps accent or mood lighting to cast a relaxing glow or highlight a favorite artwork. Don't make the mistake of leaving the bedroom entirely dark except for bedside light: too much contrast is hard on the eyes.

You'll find detailed information on lighting schemes, fixtures, and bulbs on pages 92–95. Besides general room lighting, a fixture or switch you can reach from bed is a virtual necessity. Be sure to account for the view from bed: glaring, unshielded, or high-intensity bulbs are not desirable.

Once you narrow your options, add light fixture symbols (see page 10), switches, and plug-in outlets for auxiliary lamps to your base map, with at least one switch-controlled light accessible from each doorway. Can you reach lights easily without fumbling in the dark? Have you provided sufficient light for a sitting area or walk-in closet?

It's important to remember that light-colored surfaces reflect light and dark surfaces absorb it (exceptions are very shiny, lacquerlike finishes). Fabric textures also respond to light—think of the sheen of silk or the haze of mohair. A bedroom's colors and textures interact both with daylight and with the color temperatures of the light sources you choose. Mirrors and shiny surfaces multiply light sources and add drama.

But now we're crossing the divide to that other realm of bedroom design—the world of color, pattern, and style. To learn more about these and other decorating concepts, simply turn the page.

Three Types of Lighting

Bedroom lighting needs are categorized as ambient (A), task (B), and accent (C).

DECORATING BASICS

A well-planned bedroom combines the basic elements of color, pattern, and texture with subtle design concepts to create a beautiful, balanced effect. Understanding the theory that underlies those options will help you achieve the look you want in your decorative accents, as well as overall.

ALL ABOUT COLOR

Whether or not you have strong preferences, color is undoubtedly your first consideration when planning a decor. With an understanding of the fundamentals, you'll know how to create a color scheme.

Remember that colors come and go in home decorating just as they do in fashion, so avoid trendy colors that will soon look dated. Also remember that color is enormously subjective and emotional. Consider your color likes and dislikes and those of family members who will live with the scheme you're creating. And finally, remember that guidelines are just guidelines, not hard-and-fast rules. If you want to experiment with unusual color combinations, go ahead; but take care to work with the largest samples possible before you commit yourself.

A color vocabulary. To understand and use color theory, you need to know some basic terms.

Hue is just another word for color. Every hue has a "visual temperature." Yellow, red, and orange are warm and lively; they're often referred to as advancing colors because they seem nearer than they are. Blue, green, and violet are cool and tranquil; they're called receding colors because they appear to be farther away.

Just as important as actual color is *intensity*, the degree of purity, or saturation, of color. For example, although both robin's egg and indigo are technically "blue," they differ in their intensity, or strength, of color. *Value* is the amount of light or dark in color. Adding white to a color produces a *tint*; adding black makes it a *shade*.

The color wheel. As you look at the color wheel on the facing page, remember that most colors used in decorating schemes are altered or combined in ways that soften their impact.

All color combinations and variations come from the color wheel. Although the color wheel can't dictate schemes, it can help you imagine what will happen when colors are put together.

Primary colors—red, blue, and yellow—are the source of all other colors. Primaries are powerful, usually too powerful to use full strength on such large areas as bedroom walls.

Secondary colors lie midway between the primary colors on the wheel because they're formed by combining primaries: green comes from blue and yellow, orange from yellow and red, and violet from red and blue. Secondary colors are less strong than primaries.

Intermediate colors result when you mix a primary color with an adjacent secondary color. Blue (a primary) and violet (a secondary) combine to make blue-violet, an intermediate—and so on.

Complementary colors are those opposite each other on the wheel. Red and green are complements, as are blue and orange, yellow and violet.

Tertiary and *quaternary colors* add depth and sophistication to a color scheme. Look at the color circle on the facing page and follow the arrows to make the tertiaries: green and orange make wheat, orange and violet make brick, and violet and green make slate. Note that the tertiaries have had varying amounts of white added to them. Combining tertiary colors creates quaternary colors: wheat and brick become sandstone, brick and slate become eggplant, and slate and wheat become juniper.

Neutral colors are white, black, and variations of gray. Low-intensity warm colors such as beige and ecru are also considered neutrals and are often used in understated design schemes.

Combining colors. Your bedroom's decor may already suggest a color scheme, or perhaps you have some favorite colors you want to combine. Whatever the case, understanding the three basic types of color scheme will help you devise your own. Again, keep in mind that the colors are usually softened versions of those on the wheel.

Monochromatic schemes employ one color in a variety of intensities and values. Because colors have so much in common in monochromatic schemes, rooms appear unified and harmonious.

Complementary schemes are those based on the colors opposite each other on the color wheel. They tend to be richer than monochromatic schemes because they balance warm and cool colors. These mixes can be startling or subdued: instead of violet and yellow, think about a bedroom with soft amethyst curtains and creamy walls.

Within the complementary category, there are more complex combinations. A *triad* consists of any three colors equidistant on the color wheel. A *split complement* also has three colors—one primary color plus the color on each side of its opposite; yellow plus red-violet and blue-violet is an example of a split complement.

To avoid the clash of pure opposing color, always vary the intensity, quantity, and value of complementary colors. Look carefully at fabrics with complementary schemes to see how colors are varied and balanced. Often, you can start with a well-designed fabric and use its colors to plan your color scheme.

Analogous, or related, color combinations are composed of two or more colors that lie next to each other on the color wheel. This combination results when you start with a favorite color and add related colors to it.

Color's qualities. Thinking about how the colors actually appear will make it easier for you to visualize your final results. In general, light colors are expansive, dark colors more intimate and space contracting. To increase the sense of light in a dull bedroom, use pale tints of warm or cool colors on windows and walls. To make a large room seem cozier, use rich, dark shades that draw the space in. Elsewhere in the room, be sure to repeat colors used at the bed or window to pull together and balance the scheme.

Color is also affected by the direction of light. For example, a room facing north will feel more cheerful bathed in warm color, while cool hues tone down the bright light in a west-facing room.

A ceiling painted the same color as the walls, or even lighter, helps expand space. A darker ceiling, or a ceiling color that comes down the walls a bit, visually lowers the ceiling, producing a cozier atmosphere.

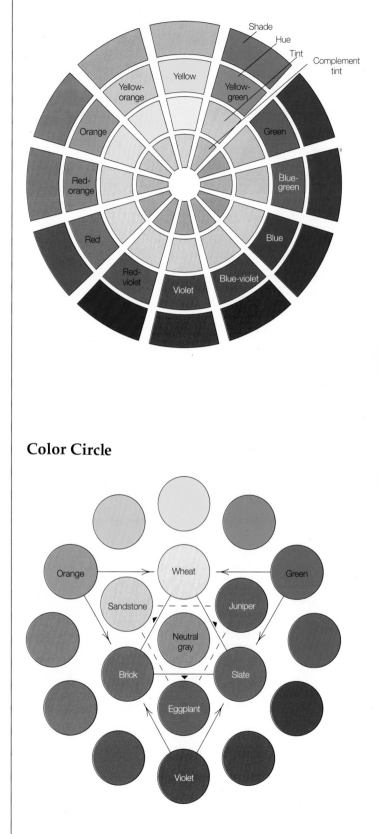

Color Wheel

Color Circle

Colors, patterns, and textures combine to form soft, muted schemes (above) or bolder, brassier palettes (facing page).

PATTERN PRINCIPLES

Pattern enriches any decorating scheme, adding depth, movement, and visual interest. But it can be tricky to use one pattern effectively, let alone combine several different patterns.

You can develop pattern confidence by following some basic principles. There are no immutable rules, but observing how patterns appear on bedroom surfaces and how they interact will make the job of selecting and combining them easier.

Keeping things in scale. The size of a pattern should correspond to the scale of the room and its detailings. Small-scale patterns are often used in cozy rooms, where their design is clearly retained and seen. Save large-scale patterns for spacious rooms; because they seem to take up space, such patterns can create the impression that a room is smaller than it actually is.

Combining different patterns. Patterns that share at least one color combine easily. One pattern may have all the colors in a scheme, another may contain just one color plus white, while a third may consist of two of the colors.

Similar patterns of different scales also combine well, such as small checks and larger plaids. Again, a common or analogous color will help tie the look together.

For decorating purposes, you can approach pattern combinations in three different ways. The first is simplicity, with unpatterned walls, windows, and furnishings—seen, for example, in the spare Shaker style as well as in more formal schemes. When you adopt this approach, let subtle textures come into play.

Another approach is to use pattern throughout—on the windows, on the walls, even on the furnishings. This all-out mix of patterns, tricky to pull off successfully, relies on making careful choices. A good rule of thumb is to use only one bold pattern in a room and use it on a large surface so that it predominates. Then add two or possibly three smaller-scale patterns, distributing them around the room to avoid pattern clusters.

A third approach is to combine pattern with plain color for a balanced look. Keeping walls plain while dressing windows in pattern draws attention to the windows and the window treatment.

THE ROLE OF TEXTURE

Shiny chintz curtains, nubby wool carpeting, richly tasseled fringe—all bedroom materials possess texture, from distinctive to subtle.

When the texture is smooth, light is reflected and colors appear lighter and more lustrous; smooth materials look cool and sophisticated.

When there's more definite texture, materials appear duller because their surfaces absorb light. For example, most window treatments with noticeable texture—such as coarse canvas or loosely woven casements—promote a casual look.

How you use texture depends, in part, on how you've used color and pattern in the room. A monochromatic color scheme with very little pattern allows for more texture than does a scheme with bold color or pattern. A masculine bedroom, for example, is a good place for neutral, subtly textured fabrics such as cotton/linen blends.

For a beautiful mix of rough and smooth surfaces throughout a room, try to introduce enough texture to create interest, but not so much that visual chaos results. And remember that patterned fabric, even if it's smooth, has a visual texture, too.

A LOOK AT DECORATING STYLES

Most home furnishings fall into one of two broad categories: traditional or contemporary. Besides denoting the period of the furnishings, the terms also refer to the decorating style. Rarely, however, is any room decorated totally in one way or the other. Instead, many people prefer what is commonly referred to as an eclectic style, one that judiciously mixes both the traditional and the contemporary.

Traditional. This is the style that's always in style. Though it's a catchall decorating term covering many period styles from different regions and countries, "traditional" does imply certain characteristics: graceful shapes, a formal look, and a quiet order. Rarely, however, are traditional schemes exact re-creations of period styles. Instead, most people choose favorite motifs, colors, and patterns from different eras.

■ *Period styles.* Among the English periods, 18th-century *Georgian* produced furniture styles that live on today—in pieces reflecting the sensibility of the great cabinetmakers of the era,

IF YOU NEED HELP

Many of us lack either the energy or the expertise to tackle a major bedroom project from start to finish. Fortunately, there's help available. The listing below covers professionals in design and construction and points out the differences among them.

Architects. Architects are state-licensed professionals with degrees in architecture. They're trained to create designs that are structurally sound, functional, and aesthetically pleasing. They know construction materials, can negotiate bids from contractors, and can supervise the work. Many architects are members of the American Institute of Architects (AIA). If stress calculations must be made, architects can make them; other professionals need state-licensed engineers to design the structure and sign the working drawings.

Interior designers. Even if you're working with an architect, you may wish to call on the services of an interior designer for finishing touches. Designers and decorators specialize in decorating and furnishing rooms and can offer fresh, innovative ideas and advice. Through their contacts, a homeowner has access to materials and products not available at the retail level. Many designers belong to the American Society of Interior Designers (ASID), a professional organization.

Some designers and decorators work on a fee basis; others charge an hourly rate. Still others will add a charge to the furnishings you buy through them. One good arrangement is to work out an hourly rate with a "not-to-exceed" clause.

Other specialists. Showroom personnel, furniture-store salespeople, building-center staff, and other retailers can help you choose and, in some cases, combine components to create a bedroom that's right for you. In fact, this kind of help may be all you need if your requirements are minor. For a larger job, check the specialist's qualifications carefully. Though some salespeople are quite capable and helpful, others may be motivated simply to sell you products.

Contractors. Contractors specialize in construction, although some also have design skills as well. General contractors may do all the work themselves, or they may assume responsibility for hiring qualified subcontractors, ordering construction materials, and seeing that the job is completed according to contract. Contractors can also secure building permits and arrange for inspections.

Chippendale, Hepplewhite, Adam, and Sheraton. In French design, elaborate scrollwork and decoration characterized *Louis XV* pieces; neoclassical *Louis XVI* furniture featured straight lines and geometric motifs.

Although early American colonists copied both English and French styles, a unique American design tradition emerged. *Early American* was a simple, unpretentious style based on European design but reinterpreted to reflect a more humble life-style. Typical designs employed stripes and plant motifs.

The graceful *Georgian* period in America featured rich hues and scenic wallpapers. It's best exemplified in the architecture and furnishings of Colonial Williamsburg.

A third American period, *Federal,* was inspired by the neoclassical revival. Walls were painted plaster or covered with formal papers from Europe and Asia. Symbols of the eagle and classical motifs were prevalent. This style's best-known example is Thomas Jefferson's home, Monticello.

■ ***Romantic.*** The *Romantic* look springs from a renewed interest in the Victorian era. Now regarded by many as excessive and flamboyant, the Victorian age made one still-popular design contribution: the production of chintz. Garden and field supplied the motifs—fruits, flowers, and leaves—in colorful, curved forms. Many of those designs appear today in lighter, brighter colors and patterns. Pretty floral wallpaper and fabric capture the charm of this style.

■ ***Country.*** The continuing popularity of the country style illustrates the perennial appeal of a simple, informal way of life. Originally, country was characterized by hand-hewn furniture, stenciled walls, and antique quilts—a return to basics.

Today's *contemporary country*, the latest version of *American country* decorating, is lighter and less representational than earlier styles, employing fewer accessories, larger and more impressionistic patterns, and lighter wood finishes.

Two 19th-century furniture styles that ran counter to Victorian excesses now infuse contemporary country with clean, spare design. The first is the Shaker style, marked by a distinctive grace and purity. The plain, pared-down pieces created by Shaker artisans possess a timeless quality; they also anticipate the functionality of 20th-century design. The second trend, derived from the Craftsman Movement, is the Mission, or Golden Oak, style. Larger and heavier than Shaker furniture, the sturdy productions of Gustav Stickley emphasized pure joinery and rectilinear design.

Several international country styles enjoy the same popularity as American country. The cottage garden and country house inspire the *English country* look, in which floral chintzes cover overstuffed sofas and chairs in rooms given to relaxed clutter. *French country*, one of the more decorative styles, features exuberant hues and patterns. Also humble in origin, it has a delightful freshness reflected in uncontrived pine furniture and colorful Provençal cottons.

■ ***Regional styles.*** Such regional styles as *Southwestern* and *Mediterranean* make use of colors and forms that harmonize with the physical environment. Walls are more often plain than patterned; palettes range from muted to vibrant hues drawn from land, sea, and sky. Art and accessories from the most formal regional style, *Oriental*, lend a romantic exoticism to traditional or contemporary settings.

Contemporary. From the curvilinear forms of Art Nouveau, the geometric patterns of Art Deco, and the functionality of the Bauhaus Movement came contemporary, or modern, interior design.

Today, the term identifies a style that's simple and strong. It's a spare look, one often described as high-tech and minimalist. Furniture is regarded more for form than decoration; brass, glass, chrome, and steel are common materials. Open plans, the absence of clutter, abundant light, and an underfurnished look all contribute to a sense of spaciousness. The palette may be neutral, pale, or bold, but the color is usually plain. When patterns appear, they tend to be abstract or geometric.

Eclectic. Just as you can blend traditional and contemporary elements for a transitional look, so, too, can you mix distinctly different periods and regions for an eclectic style. But for the result to look integrated and sophisticated, you must aim for some continuity.

One way to accomplish this is to decide on the atmosphere you want—formal or informal—and maintain that mood as you decorate. Another way to combine a variety of pieces is to repeat a particular color or pattern throughout the room.

DESIGN: KEVIN KNICKERBOCKER OF LE PETIT TRIANON

DESIGN: LOU ANN BAUER, BAUER INTERIOR DESIGN

Bedroom style may be traditional or modern, or an eclectic mix of both. The antique wicker bed (top) is the focal point of a romantic room dressed in floral-print upholstery, bedding, and window valance. In a more modern vein, a bedside decor (bottom) sets brightly colored prints and a brass lamp against the neutral, abstract backdrop of wall and night table.

ARCHITECT: REMICK ASSOCIATES

GREAT BEDROOMS

E ven a quick glance through the colorful photos in this chapter will show you that bedrooms are more than just rooms for *beds*. In addition to doubling as fireside hideaways, telecommuter offices, and home spas, they can be great occasions for dynamic designs that might not be practical or durable enough for other rooms.

You'll see bedrooms of all sizes and shapes, from economical guest rooms to huge master suites. Decorative schemes run a gamut from floral chintz to polished chrome, from rose-colored wallpaper to granite countertops. Don't worry if your available space or budget doesn't seem to fit the bill: many of these ideas can be scaled down effectively.

Most of the photos featured here illustrate overall design solutions or finishing touches. For details on specific products and materials, see "A Shopper's Guide," beginning on page 69.

Decidedly modern, this spacious master suite's U-shaped layout includes garden access, built-in seating, and a bedroom office on the far side of the two-sided fireplace. Textured concrete, copper soffits, and tightly woven wool carpet complete the picture.

An elegant four-poster bed is one focal point, the fireplace a second in this comfortable master bedroom off a central hallway. White-lacquered cabinets offer plenty of storage capacity while maintaining a cleanly styled surface.

CLASSIC OPTIONS

Since your master bedroom is a private space, let it express whatever mood you like. If it's sizable, consider multiuse options (would you like a fireside sitting area?) and display alcoves. Otherwise, start by locating the bed, then incorporate hardworking storage. And remember, introducing new colors or textures can totally transform a dull room.

Ample space allows multi-use floor plans and furnishings options. At left, the gently bowed windows form the backdrop for a sitting area next to the bed. Touches of black add drama to a soothing neutral color scheme that unites all the elements in the room. Above, a serene master retreat balances large-scaled pieces like this handsome burled armoire and king-size four-poster bed with a soft floral chintz and cheerful plaid to set an elegant tone. A comfortable chair and ottoman create a cozy reading corner.

CLASSIC

OPTIONS

This small, second-story bedroom is stretched and brightened with high skylights, transoms, and single-light doors, offering an intimate sense of the surrounding woods. Compact built-ins flank the doors, which open to a space-enhancing pocket deck.

To retain the look of the Texas Hill Country farmhouses that inspired this new homestead, the walls in the master bedroom are vernacular stone. Colorful bedding echoes the palette used elsewhere in the house and brightens the intimate space.

A king-size bed can overpower a typical bedroom. In this remodel the entire room design was adjusted to compensate for the bed's scale: The ceiling is vaulted to 12 feet for spaciousness, and the wall behind the headboard is 9 feet high. Built-in bookcases on either side extend 24 inches from the wall, further minimizing the size of the bed.

A corner of a spare bedroom does double duty as a quiet retreat for reading. A 5-foot-wide bookcase along one wall offers extensive storage and also serves as a focal point for the room. Add a comfortable chair, good lighting, and a spot for casual dining, puzzles, and games, and the room assumes a new purpose.

DESIGNER: MARILYN RIDING DESIGN

THE MASTER SUITE

Maybe the kids have moved out and there's extra space, or maybe you just need a buffer zone from kids who are definitely *there*. The solution could be a new addition up or out. Or, it might simply be a matter of knocking down an existing wall. Linked-use areas compose the suite; transitions tie zones together and determine the feel—open and flowing or more specifically compartmentalized.

Master suites come in single-room versions, too. In this open plan, bath fixtures are nestled behind a room-dividing knee wall; easy-to-clean tiles echo the ruddy colors of the bedroom rug and pillows, linking the areas visually.

DESIGN: COURTYARD COLLECTION. ARCHITECT: JACK BUKTENICA ASSOCIATES

The spacious multiroom floor plan on the facing page unites sleeping, sitting, and bathing areas in one gracefully styled suite. An overview across the bed (left) shows a private sitting room on the left, a makeup area at right. A view from the makeup area (facing page, top right) features one of two his-and-her vanity areas, with a whirlpool tub beyond. From the tub, it's a short walk to a glassblock walk-in shower (facing page, top left).

ARCHITECT: VICTOR H. LEE

The master wing addition shown here is almost a separate pavilion, standing 68 inches from the rest of the original house and connected to it only by an isthmus-like vestibule, above. At right, a barrel vault stretches above the patio entry to the room.

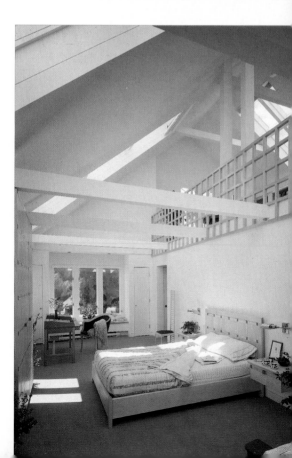

INTERIOR DESIGN: KARIN THOMAS

Some bedrooms have spacious open ceilings, and some have lofts. This master suite sports both. The main sleeping area features a built-in bed, storage wall, compact desk, and easy chair. Upstairs, the loft area houses a private study equipped with chairs, bookcases, and—for when all that reading requires a rest—a built-in whirlpool tub.

THE MASTER
SUITE

DESIGN: JOE TERRELL

Bedroom suites can link any number of specialty areas in one continuous flow of space. The suite shown below features a stepped glass-block divider between bed and bath, with a black whirlpool tub on the bedroom side. The exercise room at right, outfitted for action, is just a few brisk strides from the sleeping quarters.

DESIGNER: CATHY NASON ASID INTERIOR DESIGN

DESIGNER: FONTENOT DESIGNS

The dressing room above links a master bedroom with the bath proper: its amenities include elegant built-ins with lots of nooks and crannies, handy mirrors, a chair for pulling on socks or shoes, and warm carpeting for bathers' chilly toes.

DESIGN: THOMAS BARTLETT INTERIORS

A consistent flow of decorative materials helps tie a bath area to the bedroom beyond. At left, the daybed, double sinks, and vanity form a comparatively "public" transition zone to private bath and toilet areas.

GREAT BEDROOMS **35**

FOR KIDS ONLY

Personality, durability, and adaptability are key checkpoints in design for kids' rooms. The room should be an expression of the child's identity, not yours. But children change, so you need to think ahead: will the design be easy to modify in a few years? Is there room for storage, study, animal or doll collections, or a wrestling match? For a slew of inspiring ideas, see the *Southern Living* book *Ideas For Great Kids' Rooms.*

A cheery nursery area in the foreground steps up to the master bedroom beyond, providing a close—but not too close—link between infant and parents. As the child grows and moves to independent quarters, the nursery will become part of an adult master suite.

Here are two looks at sophisticated styling for kids, both from the same house. The menagerie of animal prints in the boy's bedroom at left offers a playful background. Below, the delicate pink toile wallpaper in the girl's room and painted antique bed set an old-fashioned, feminine mood. The furnishings of both rooms will keep their appeal as the children get older.

Customized beds anchor one-of-a-kind rooms. At right, a junior farm-hand would love droll decor that pays homage to the holstein. The barn serves as a headboard and as a storage chest. Below is a goal-oriented bedroom for a child that lives and sleeps soccer. The goalpost headboard is constructed of PVC pipe and a small soccer net. A school locker, available in specialty catalogs, serves as a bedside bookshelf.

DESIGN: JUVENILE LIFESTYLES, INC.

DESIGN: BUFFY HARGETT

This fun-filled, multifunctional loft unit contains a rooftop bed, an entertainment center built into the stairway, fenced-in toy storage under the window box, and a private play-house around back.

A bright blast of high-octane red brightens an otherwise restrained decor, courtesy of a freestanding gas pump and soft-drink machine.

GREAT BEDROOMS **39**

A Murphy bed can bring whimsy, nostalgia, and practicality to a part-time bedroom. On the facing page, the Murphy is shown both down and up. Library shelves remain undisturbed; when the bed is closed, painted trompe l'oeil books maintain a studious front.

The cushy daybed in this versatile study provides a retreat from work as well as accommodation for overnight guests. A mahogany desk is fully outfitted as a home office.

HARDWORKING GUEST ROOMS

These days, a spare bedroom rarely means spare *space*. Home offices, entertainment systems, and sewing centers all crowd its stage after the guest leaves. Built-ins and pullouts make maximum use of small footprints; consider a Murphy bed, or let twin beds double as couches with comfy pillows. Remember your guests, too: a night table, closet space, and night lighting are welcoming touches.

ARCHITECT: CLEMENS BRUNS SCHAUB

A guest bedroom needn't be the stepchild of the house. This one lives much larger than its 12- by 12-foot dimensions, thanks to a thoughtful furniture arrangement and 12-foot-high ceilings. Tall windows over the bed and a dramatic painted finish on the walls enhance the room's spaciousness and style.

In a guest room, an arched opening frames a reading nook large enough to double as a child's bed. Measuring 3 feet 4 inches deep by 6 feet 8 inches long, the built-in offers plenty of space for a toddler to stretch out and take a nap or for an adult to curl up with a book. Deep drawers below the window seat are another added benefit.

The two beds (opposite page, top) can move together to create a king-sized one (bottom) by making changes in linens and in furniture choice and placement, a useful option in a spare bedroom.

SERIOUS STORAGE

Bedroom storage is crucial, and it can offer great design opportunities. Do you want sleek built-ins or freestanding antiques? A walk-in dressing room or a capacious armoire? Cabinets, drawers, shelves, bins, racks, pullouts, hooks, and pegs all help. And don't forget storage headboards, under-bed drawers, and rollouts. In a pinch, can seldom-used items be moved to the bath, hallway, or attic?

DESIGN: JACOBSON, SILVERSTEIN & WINSLOW ARCHITECTS/PAUL WINANS CONSTRUCTION, INC.

A striking cedar storage wall divides the room and also works as a headboard. The cabinets face a grooming corridor with built-in sink and granite countertops.

Seamless, white-lacquered bedroom built-ins team copious drawers and doors with display niches and decorative uplighting. The double doors slide back on heavy-duty guides, revealing a coffee bar and compact sink.

ARCHITECT: ROBERT H. WATERMAN / WATERMAN & SUN.
INTERIOR DESIGNER: ROBERT W. MILLER, ASID / FLEGEL'S

Is it a bookshelf or a ladder? The shelving unit attached to this storage wall is designed to double as access to the sleeping loft. Miniature shelves in the corner reclaim unused space for display.

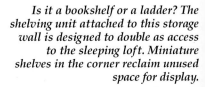

SERIOUS
STORAGE

INTERIOR DESIGN: ROBERT CURRIE

ARCHITECT: GEOFFREY BUTLER

Organize, organize, organize! The walk-in alcove at right features a built-in storage wall combining large drawers below with generous cubbyholes above. The custom-crafted drawers shown below glide out to provide easy at-a-glance access to small items like jewelry and neckties. The hardworking double doors shown above do double duty as shelves that swing open to reveal a walk-in closet.

DESIGNER: MARILYN RIDING DESIGN

ARCHITECT: ROBERT LUCHETTI

Twin towers of a custom maple headboard stairstep high above the carpeted bed platform, incorporating the functions of bedside tables without the usual clutter. They form an almost sculptural statement.

All the furniture for a multifunctional room is contained within the confines of this extensive wall system, with its array of specialized components and accessories. It incorporates a fold-down bed, a nightstand, shelving, lighting, a mirror, drawers, space for audio and video gear, and a home office that includes a large pull-down desk.

DESIGN: EURODESIGN, LTD.

A black-rimmed, freestanding storage unit separates the bathroom, with primary color accents, from an adjacent bedroom. It's like a kitchen island transported to the sleeping quarters.

DESIGNER: CAROLYN VAN LANG

ARCHITECT: J. ALLEN SAYLES

This passagelike dressing area forms a transition zone between bedroom and bath; the owners wanted a master suite feel but didn't have space for a separate dressing room. Built-in cabinets have plenty of drawers, pegs, cubbyholes, and adjustable shelves; a lower section becomes a makeup counter.

SITTING PRETTY

If space allows, a sitting area brings a comfortable touch to your bedroom plan. Do you want built-in window seating or separate pieces? An area near the bed or one in a detached alcove? A table provides a platform for coffee and the Sunday paper. A thick rug adds sound insulation as well as softness underfoot. Good lighting is a must. And a fireplace or woodstove offers cozy cheer on winter nights.

Antiqued French-style benches with upholstered seats make a comfortable perch at the foot of the bed. The benches are also a handy spot for the bedspread if you take it off at night. An oversize armchair with ottoman and table in the far corner invites reading and relaxing.

Dressed in dark rose with white crown moldings and trim, this bedroom gains formality from a symmetrically arranged sitting area. Matching armchairs and built-in window seats flank a central fireplace.

A walk-in bay sheds light and stretches space for an adjacent sitting area. A side table, good reading lamp, and footrest turn a couple of chairs into an appealing destination. An area rug helps define the spot.

THE BEDROOM OFFICE

Two minuses to a bedroom office are clutter and, if a nonworking partner is nearby, sound and light when he or she wants to sleep. Modular bins, drawers, pop-up printer stands, and the like can help hide the office mess. For the partner's sake, buffer the desk area with a knee wall, room divider, or sliding doors. Don't forget electrical needs such as power strips, a fax hookup, and good light fixtures.

DESIGNER: CHER STONE BEALL

Once the living and dining rooms of a cottage, these two rooms are now the master bedroom and office-sitting area. The owner recycled a potting bench for her desk.

One corner of this home office is defined by angled walls that wrap around the built-in desk. The no-space-wasted remodel took advantage of an unnecessarily wide bedroom hall and also borrowed a sliver of space from an adjacent patio. The ceiling beam marks the location of the original outside wall.

DESIGN: EURODESIGN, LTD.

ARCHITECT: PATRICIA OWEN

Open for business, the workspace above emerges from high-efficiency cabinetry. When work is done, the printer shelf rides into the cabinet on tracks and a retractable door swings down. The keyboard tucks away and folding doors conceal the monitor.

ARCHITECT: STEVE ROAKE, AIA

An office that's attached to but separate from the bedroom provides the best of both worlds: it gives the user the quiet and privacy of the master bedroom but can be sealed off when a partner is sleeping. When it's break time, the home executive can lounge on the couch by the fireplace.

INTERIOR DESIGNER: STEVEN STEIN/MILLER-STEIN

DESIGN: GREG ERICKSON, DESIGN CABINET SHOWROOM

Home entertainment systems may be hidden or showcased. Above, the silver screen drops from a floating soffit, then retracts out of sight when not in use; projection equipment is housed at the foot of the bed. The striking cherry wall system shown at left combines elegant detailing with a built-in monitor, speakers, audio and video components, and other amenities: note the wine cooler and ice-maker at far left.

A MEDIA EVENT

Gone is the era of the bedroom TV propped on a chair or chest. Now rear-projection TV monitors, remote pull-down screens, laser discs, and surround-sound speakers abound. Do you want to locate your home theater in the master bedroom or in a less used guest room? Do you prefer discreet built-ins or a striking wall system? Couch potatoes (bed spuds, too) may want a "master remote" that integrates multiple machines.

ARCHITECT: HEATHER MCKINNEY

When closed, this pine wardrobe (shown below) looks like a typical bedroom feature. The armoire opens (right) to reveal a television and a hidden ship's ladder that leads to an attic study. The door on the left features a false-fronted drawer; the right-hand section features a deep drawer for storage.

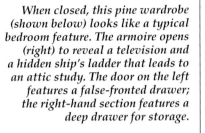

ON THE SURFACE

Walls, ceilings, floors, and bedding can form a subtle backdrop or make a bolder statement. Do you want the furnishings complementary or contrasting? The master bedroom is often an occasion for a splurge of luxury. Hard-use kids' rooms require durability. And guest-room treatments must be flexible, more neutral, and, frequently, economical.

Wall color and choice of fabrics make a dramatic difference in a room's ambience. Lush fabrics, like soft chenille, silk, and tapestry, create a sense of luxury in the spacious master bedroom above. Walls are painted dark sage green to show off the sheen of the bedding and upholstery as well as the gilded accessories. At left, a canopy bed in dark mahogany delineates an otherwise serene scheme of creams and pale greens on the walls, bedding, and on the classic camelback sofa that anchors the foot of the bed.

A botanical theme envelopes this master bedroom, tying it to the woodland scene just beyond the deck. A light palette prevails, emphasized by airy panels of white fabric hanging at each corner of the bed.

Eclectic designs can maintain calm while using bold strokes of color, pattern, and texture. The antique screen above forms a serene and shimmering backdrop to the tailored bed and brightly patterned bedding. At left, crossed polo mallets hung on the wall above a sleigh bed, honor the owner's favorite sport and make an unusual, but complementary addition to the room's dark wood and brass accents.

DESIGNER: DANNY HARTLEY

Striking blends of color, line, and texture come into play below in a rough-combed concrete headboard with glowing glass block, silk bed cover, and pearly streaked, glazed walls. At right, a monochromatic color scheme and a mix of antiques create modern sophistication in this master bedroom. When gilded, glazed, and upholstered, an antique door surround is transformed from an architectural fragment to a stunning headboard for a king-size bed.

DESIGN: OZ DESIGNS / LINDA OSBORN

DESIGN: LOU ANN BAUER, BAUER INTERIOR DESIGNS

In country style, this simple room has shiplap knotty pine paneling on the walls, beaded strips on the ceiling, and wide planks on the floor. It's also fitted with pine shelves and pegs.

Surfaces provide an unlimited array of color and pattern combinations. Above, colors and patterns of bedding and pillows are picked up by plush purple carpeting and a printed Roman shade. Decorative wall glazing is set off by clean white moldings and ceiling paint.

ARCHITECT: MARGO JONES

Contemporary rooms can maintain a distinct sense of style with neutral color schemes. Above, a comfortable bedroom, a cheery two-sided fireplace, and a whirlpool tub are wrapped in white with contrasting granite. At left, handpainted marble-look wallpaper curves around corners and holds varied light and dark surfaces in a unified ambience.

This manufactured bow window brings in plenty of light, stretches room space, and lends a graceful curve to a bedroom design. Built-in benches with handy storage and display bins below add a finishing touch.

Morning light streams into a master bedroom. An arched window and transoms keep the room bright as the sun climbs toward midday.

LIGHT EFFECTS

Windows bring light, views, and ventilation to your bedroom; they also affect its personality. Would you prefer a big-view window wall or small, discreet clerestories? Skylights and roof windows can bring daylight deep into a room without disturbing privacy. And don't forget doors; fitted with clear or diffused glazing, they can serve as though they were windows, too. New glazing options and thermal-break frames help make openings energy-efficient as well as beautiful.

ARCHITECT: SARAH HOUSE TATE

Windows flood the bedroom with sunlight and offer panoramic views to the rear garden. The green floral fabric suits the scene.

LIGHT
EFFECTS

ARCHITECT: HOUSE + HOUSE OF SAN FRANCISCO

At right, a glass-block wall provides an elegant, textured backdrop and lets watery daylight in, while masking views to and from the street.

WINDOW TREATMENT: ROSSETTI & CORRIEA

A second-story or attic bedroom can acquire new space, light, and interest with the addition of a dormer, large or small. This small dormer's wallpaper pattern varies subtly from that on surrounding walls, giving the sloping surface a lighter look.

A pivoting, crank-operated roof window brings a striking view—and welcome ventilation—into a small upstairs bedroom.

A bank of traditional arched windows gives a classic feel to this bedroom sitting area and supplies fresh air, too. Sheer diffusing screens soften incoming light and ensure privacy; clear glass above eye level allows views out.

DESIGN: COURTYARD COLLECTION

Double doors open to a sunny expanse of verdant lawn and tall trees, bringing light and warmth to the master bedroom. They also make a very attractive frame for the view.

I NSIDE OUT

Nothing stretches bedroom space like a nearby pocket deck or patio. Maybe there's an underused side yard nearby or, for a second-story room, the roof of an attached garage. A platform with container plants, a trellis, and perhaps a privacy wall are all you'll need. French doors are the traditional link to the outdoors, though today's sliders are attractively designed and can often be more efficient.

ARCHITECTS: GORDON AND SUSAN WITTENBERG, MARK OBERHOLZER, WITTENBERG PARTNERSHIP

Just steps above the master suite is a treetop deck that's a private spot to drink morning coffee and watch the sun rise. Levers on the French doors were set low for convenience. The decking is wood-plastic composite, an alternative to wood that is a soothing neutral color and doesn't rot.

Occupants enjoy fresh air and unlimited circulation when the walls roll back and open the core of this compact house to blue skies. The folding doors, housed in 24-inch-thick wall extensions, operate on sturdy overhead tracks.

GREAT BEDROOMS **67**

A SHOPPER'S GUIDE

Y ou've explored a wide range of design ideas. Now, perhaps, you're ready to get down to bedroom shopping. This chapter will help you find your way through such diverse realms as beds, built-ins, closet accessories, wall coverings, windows and skylights, flooring, and lighting.

As we go along, we also spotlight decorative window treatments and survey the exploding options in home electronics available for master bedrooms or guestroom/den setups.

When it's time to make choices, use this information to help you establish an overview. Then gather up your base map (see page 10) or a diagram of the room and head for the showrooms. Most wallpaper, fabric, and even flooring retailers will be happy to provide swatches or samples for you to view in your own home—and in your room's own light.

A black steel canopy bed is set off by pale striped painted walls, a 19th-century pine storage chest, and a broad-shouldered mahogany and chestnut antique chair. Light streams through the gauzy curtains made of wedding-dress lace.

THE NOT-SO-BASIC BED

What is and is not customary and convenient for sleeping depends on where in the world you live. In Japan, you unfold a futon at night, then store it at dawn. In the South Pacific, you retire to a hammock.

The Western bed tends to be less portable, and also somewhat heftier. In Europe, the bed was for many centuries a prized status symbol, and the bigger (and more thickly canopied) the better. However, those of us who need to make the most of less-than-palatial floor space will probably want something more modest.

Here's a survey of standard (and some not-so-standard) bed designs, plus a brief look at mattresses, bases, bedding, and pillows.

The familiar bed

Today, standard steel frames are most frequently used with box spring and mattress sets (see page 75). Casters, flat guides, or barrel-shaped rollers allow you to move the bed around, though they all are likely to leave marks on the rug.

Many brass and wooden beds are constructed as one unit, in which headboard, footboard, and side rails all fit together.

A steel bed frame, on the other hand, is purchased separately from the headboard. A freestanding headboard can be used, or you can connect the headboard of your choice to the frame.

Many steel frames have headboard-attachment brackets welded or riveted to them. With bed frames that have no attachment brackets, you can use adapter plates to attach the headboard.

A bevy of special beds

In addition to the tried-and-true bed frame, you have a wide choice of other designs. Here's a sampler of styles.

Brass and other metals. Metal bedsteads became common in the second half of the 19th century. Rolled-steel and cast-iron beds with ornamental brass joints were popular, as were bed frames of brass-wrapped steel tubing. Very few beds were made of solid brass, which is heavy and not as strong as steel.

Basic Bed Frames

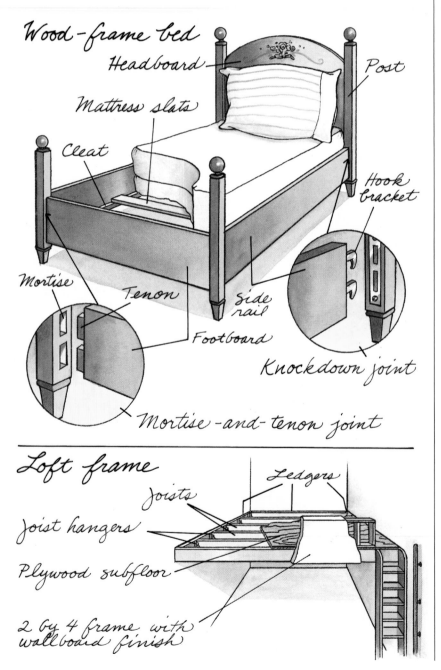

Wood-frame bed
Headboard
Post
Mattress slats
Cleat
Hook bracket
Mortise
Tenon
Side rail
Footboard
Knockdown joint
Mortise-and-tenon joint

Loft frame
Ledgers
Joists
Joist hangers
Plywood subfloor
2 by 4 frame with wallboard finish

DESIGN: THOMAS BARTLETT INTERIORS

It's two beds in one. Side-by-side brass canopy frames are teamed with textured muslin bed curtains and a single king-size mattress. Soft-hued, floral-printed wallpaper forms a rich backdrop.

ARCHITECT AND INTERIOR DESIGN: J. REED ROBBINS

A modern metal bed's wrought-iron styling sets the tone for a minimalist master-suite design; the sculptural lines repeat in night tables, chairs, plant stand, and accessories.

THE NOT-SO-BASIC

BED

To refurbish an older iron or steel frame, have it sandblasted to remove paint and rust, then paint it yourself or have it enameled. Solid brass parts and brass-clad metal tubing should be polished professionally—it's a difficult and time-consuming job to attempt yourself.

Canopy beds. Descendants of the canopied, curtained beds of medi-eval castles are still with us, both in re-creations of the originals and in modernized versions. The great appeal of a canopy bed is its room-within-a-room ambience—the cozy, private enclosure it creates. The drawback to a canopy bed is its size, real and apparent. These beds require a high ceiling and can easily overwhelm a small room.

Today, bed frames with bedposts and canopies come in many styles and materials, from sleek metal to geometric rattan or carved wood.

Fabric can embellish canopy beds as linings, valances, curtains, and draperies. Delicate eyelet lace or netting lightens the appearance of a large canopy bed; heavier fabrics give a snug feeling and can even serve their original purpose—shutting out drafts.

Adjustable beds and hospital beds. After hospital stays, people sometimes miss the versatility of the beds they used there. To enjoy such fine-tuned comfort at home, you can

DESIGN: DIANE CLOOS

ARCHITECT: DICK REED. INTERIOR DESIGN: ROBIN WHITTEN

The three beds on this page are about as varied a group as can be. Above, a metal-frame Murphy bed swings down from its hiding place in a guest room's book-lined walls. At top right, the wooden loft platform with fluffy futons forms an elevated retreat. At lower right, the room-within-a-room cedar enclosure provides built-in storage behind its crafted facade.

purchase a bed at a hospital-supply outlet. Furniture stores often carry adjustable beds, which are less institutional-looking modifications of hospital beds. These usually bend at the head and foot but don't elevate.

Platform beds. This style is raised one or more steps up from floor level, and it may incorporate storage space below. Whether you decide on a built-in platform or a movable one nailed together out of lumber or plywood, it can be surfaced with wood,

wallboard, or even carpeting to match or contrast with the wall or floor.

Because the mattress sits directly on the platform instead of on a box spring, a platform bed is often firmer and lower than other beds.

Loft beds. Another use of the term "platform" refers to a high, loftlike structure reached by a ladder or stairs. Such a structure can save space dramatically in a high-ceilinged room and allow working, storage, or relaxing space below.

If the loft is freestanding, it can be built from either plywood or a combination of sturdy posts and structural floor framing. A wall-attached unit (shown on page 70) is like a second floor suspended above the existing one.

Bunk beds and trundle beds. As beds to serve guests, bunk beds and trundles save space during the day, yet give a restful night's sleep. Either is also a workable every-night bed, if you're gymnastically inclined.

A Western ranch was the inspiration for the theme room above, featuring rough-hewn pine bunk beds, a leather easy chair, and outdoor gear including a lasso and fishing creel; the upper bunk is accessed by a sturdy log ladder. At left, a built-in captain's bed makes a snug sleeping nook for a child, and shelves at the head and foot hold all the nighttime necessities.

A SHOPPER'S GUIDE   **73**

Bolsters, neck rolls, puffs—whatever the shape, you can never have too many pillows. Use them to add soft-ness, literally and figuratively, to your bedroom design.

Bedding options offer both creature comfort and decorative oppor-tunities. Quilts, comforters, sheets, shams, bed skirts, and pillows come in a wide array of colors, shapes, and sizes.

BEDDING COURTESY OF LACEY ELLEN OF BENICIA

Bunk beds are typically used in kids' rooms, where a certain sense of adventure is often welcome. The upper bunk should have a sturdy guardrail—one on each side, if the bed is not placed against a wall.

A trundle bed, normally the size of a twin bed, wheels out from underneath another bed to sleep a sibling or an overnight guest. The mattress stays flat, so it remains comfortable longer than one that must be folded and compressed.

The futon. Whether it's rolled out at night on the floor or set atop a wooden slat frame, a futon makes an effective bed for studios or other small spaces. In Japan, the futon mattress was originally fashioned from cotton batting inside a heavy fabric casing; Western futons usually have an added layer of foam and/or other padding for greater longevity.

The Murphy bed idea. Patented in 1905, the original Murphy bed was such a success that its name has become a generic term. The classic Murphy pivoted up into a closet, was reasonably easy to operate, and freed floor space for other daytime uses. Manufacturers today make Murphy-type beds that tilt into bookcases and various cabinet frameworks. Some beds are hinged at the head, others at the side.

Beneath it all: the mattress

Though the style of the bed sets the tone for your bedroom, it's the mattress and its foundation that have the most to do with how comfortably you sleep.

Basically, the choice is between an innerspring mattress and a foam mattress. The mattress, in turn, must rest on some sort of foundation—often, though not necessarily, a box spring.

Innerspring mattresses. These mattresses house springs connected in various ways (see drawing at right). Generally, pocketed springs are considered best. Whatever the spring design, look for more than 100 coils in a crib mattress, more than 200 in a twin mattress, and more than 300 in a larger model. A high count isn't the whole story, though. Wire gauge is also important: the lower the number, the stronger the wire, with 13 the heaviest gauge and 21 the lightest.

Also, the more layers of quality cushioning and insulation that are added, the more comfortable the mattress will prove. If you'd like a cushy surface coupled with firm support below, look for a "soft top" model.

Foam mattresses. A high-quality foam mattress is just as good as a well-constructed innerspring mattress and can be made to fit an odd-size custom or antique bed. Your dealer can easily cut or seam pieces to fit your exact requirements.

Generally, the higher the density, the better the foam. Be sure to get a minimum density of at least 1.15 pounds per cubic foot in a crib mattress or 2 pounds per cubic foot in an adult-size mattress.

Box springs and mattress bases. Innerspring mattresses can be used on many kinds of bases and frames. As a rule, the more solid the base, the longer the life of the mattress.

A simple sheet of plywood, or even the floor, makes an adequate mattress support. Besides promoting air circulation, the only advantages of a box spring or other mattress base are giving additional resiliency to the mattress and raising its height.

Water beds. Design has taken great steps forward since these beds were introduced in the 1960s. Newer water mattresses come with a solidly comfortable foam edge; others use an air baffle or rows of springs along the mattress perimeter, and baffles of various designs inside some mattresses slow down wave motion. A polyurethane liner contains the water in case of a leak.

Mattresses Exposed

Open springs

Continuous springs

Pocketed springs

Laminated foam

Water bed

Mattress pad

Cushioned perimeter

Water mattress

Heater

Safety liner

STORAGE FURNITURE

When you're planning storage, take a look at your bedroom with fresh eyes, using the guidelines on page 13 as a starting point. Perhaps you like the informal look of simple bins and baskets. Or you may prefer antique furniture and cabinetry. In any case, efficiency should be your goal.

Clutter-busting closets

You can never be too rich or too thin—or have too much closet space. We can't help you with the first two, but there are a few things we can point out about the third.

Specialized stores and mail-order outlets can help you find your own closet hardware and accessories. And if you don't want to do anything but write the check, there are talented designers who can help you take advantage of the numerous closet systems available. Check your Yellow Pages under "Closet Designers."

Hangers, bins, and bags. Take stock of your wardrobe, and you'll quickly realize that some things are longer than others, that some things are better stored folded than hung, and that lots of things get lost. The old adage "Out of sight, out of mind" could have been written about the contents of your closet.

The way to keep all those formerly lost items from disappearing again is to put them where you'll see them. The photo at left shows a collection of storage retrofits for existing spaces.

Doubling up clothes rods is a key space-saver (in a child's closet you can even triple up). Position the top rod 6½ to 7 feet off the floor and the lower one 3 to 3½ feet up; err on the high side. A single rod is usually just under 6 feet off the floor; you'll probably still need a short length of single rod for coats and the like.

What about systems? The most basic system—the home-center standard that's easiest to work with and offers the most options for the do-it-yourselfer—uses coated wire for rods, shelves, and accessories. Various component kits allow you to fit the system to virtually any closet; you can turn corners, stop short of side walls, even make the unit free-standing. Other widely available organizers use coated steel planks, wood, melamine-surfaced particleboard, or MDF (medium-density fiberboard).

Many of the MDF-based systems sport those ubiquitous rows of "system 32" holes up the sides of their panels, allowing each module to be fitted with shelves, drawers, doors, or

Hang-ups are a good thing—at least when it comes to organizing closets. The bins and baskets help, too. Products like these allow you to retrofit existing space for maximum storage potential.

Whether your style is formal or casual, you'll find appropriate closet systems at specialty shops and home centers. The rich, European-looking dressing room at top was custom designed with acrylic dust doors and invisible hardware. The kids'-room unit at left sports flexible, easy-to-clean laminate components. The slide-out shoe drawer above is one of many system options you can add.

anything else that can plug into the holes. You can also change components around when you need to.

You can have any degree of finish you like, from purely utilitarian up to fine cabinet quality. In fact, a well-finished closet can be one of the high points when you show off your house—especially to a friend who still tosses things in and then chancily crams the door shut.

Starting from scratch? Few homes, new or old, have enough closet space. But if you have the floor space, you can construct a built-in closet that looks as though it's been there from the beginning.

You can frame a closet in one of two ways: by using standard 2 by 4 wall framing and the wall covering of your choice or by installing floor-to-ceiling cabinets built from hardwood plywood or fiberboard. Both methods are shown on the facing page.

The 2 by 4 frame is the simplest to build and blends right in with the room. Cabinets, on the other hand, create a "custom woodwork" look and allow a number of design options, such as split-level compartments and built-in drawers.

In general, closets need to be about 24 to 27 inches deep inside (with the rods set 12 inches from the back wall). You can squeeze it a little tighter—but don't. It's good to have some room around your clothes so you can move them easily.

Both these walk-in closets combine generous storage capacity with great looks. The white laminate unit at top presents a seamless Euro-style face of flush-front doors and drawers; mirrors add a space-stretching touch to an otherwise blank wall. The built-ins at right, wrapped in beautiful bird's-eye maple, combine copious drawers and open shelving; a space-saving pullout tames the shoe collection.

DESIGN: STEPHEN W. SANBORN

Storage furniture: unfitted or modular?

A visit to a retail furniture showroom will unveil a surprising range of ready-made storage and display furnishings. You'll discover state-of-the-art European wall systems, Shaker-style media centers, French étagères, and many styles of chests and cabinets that can be used individually or in groupings to meet your exact needs. The quality of the piece is generally reflected in the joinery and detailing of drawers, doors, and similar parts.

You can buy storage furniture at furniture stores, department stores, and designer showrooms. Some furnishings are sold through mail-order catalogs. For complete media centers or furniture to organize electronic gear, visit quality home-electronics stores. And if you look around a bit, you can find ready-made storage solutions in other places—antique stores, unfinished furniture stores, even office-supply stores.

It's easy to understand the appeal of a modular system. You can combine shelves, cabinets, drawers, and other components to fit your exact needs and space requirements; and when you move, you can pack up the pieces and take them along with you.

Most large manufacturers offer scores of components, accessories, and finishes. Components often include several cabinet types, a variety of shelves, several different doors, desk units, drawers, even fold-up beds. In addition, many systems offer a range of special accessories, such as record racks, swiveling pullouts for television sets, wine racks, and other helpful organizers.

Some modular systems are largely preassembled; all you do is mount the components on supports. With others, you may need to install door fronts on cabinets. Still others require that you assemble everything, even the drawers.

Built-in Closets

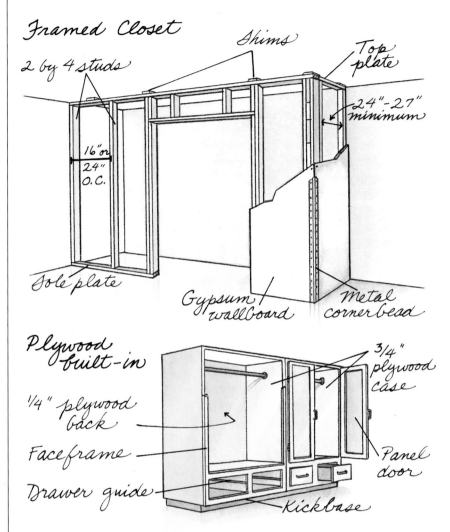

Framed Closet — 2 by 4 studs — Shims — Top plate — 24"–27" minimum — 16" or 24" O.C. — Sole plate — Gypsum wallboard — Metal cornerbead

Plywood built-in — 1/4" plywood back — Face frame — Drawer guide — 3/4" plywood case — Panel door — Kickbase

DESIGN: JACOBSON, SILVERSTEIN & WINSLOW ARCHITECTS/
PAUL WINANS CONSTRUCTION, INC.

ARCHITECT: ARCHITECTURAL KITCHENS & BATHS

Built-ins pack plenty of service behind innocently blank fronts. Ties and belts (left) are sorted behind cedar panel doors; an ironing board (right) swings down when needed from a recessed wall cabinet.

Manufactured cabinets

Factory-made cabinets, the kind typically used in kitchens and bathrooms, are an important option to consider when you're planning permanent, built-in storage for your bedroom.

Sold through kitchen-cabinet dealers, manufactured cabinets come in many styles, from relatively inexpensive stock modules to high-end custom creations.

Traditional American cabinets mask the front edges of each box with a 1 by 2 faceframe. Because the faceframe covers the edges, thin or low-quality panels can be used for the sides, which lowers the price. But the frame takes up space; it also reduces the size of the openings, so drawers and slide-out accessories must be significantly smaller than the cabinet's width. Hinges for faceframe cabinets are usually visible from the front.

On European, or frameless, cabinets, the raw front edges of the basic box are banded with narrow trim strips. Overlay doors and drawer fronts usually fit to within ¼ inch of one another, revealing a thin sliver of the edge trim. Interior components such as drawers can be sized almost to the full interior dimensions of the box. And the door hinges are invisible.

Stock cabinet widths are typically 9 to 48 inches, increasing in 3-inch increments. Base cabinets, 24 inches deep and 34½ inches high, are made to fit under counters, so they may not have a top panel. Wall cabinets are 12 inches deep and 12 to 60 inches high. Wardrobe, bookcase, and hutch-style cabinets are 18 to 24 inches deep and 30 to 96 inches high.

Though generally more expensive, custom shops can match old cabinets, build to odd configurations, and accommodate details that can't be handled by stock dealers.

Storage can be supplied by efficient built-ins or freestanding, often eclectic, pieces. Behind a series of double doors at right are three closets that eliminate the need for dressers. The old wooden armoire at lower right has lots of presence—and resides in its own alcove. The flea-market dresser below was revived with artist's acrylics, sealed with clear varnish, then pressed into service.

DECORATIVE ARTIST: N. E. LARKIN

W

Textile wall coverings come in many colors and textures, from casual to formal. They're usually made of cotton, linen, or other natural plant fibers or of polyester, often bonded to a paper-type backing. Grass cloth is a favorite among textile wall coverings; hemp is similar but has thinner fibers. Keep in mind that most textiles fray easily and are not washable, though most will accept a spray-on stain repellent.

Hand-screened papers, though more expensive than the majority of other wallpapers, have a unique three-dimensional appearance and can offer a wealth of color in just a single pattern.

Foils and other *metallics* can brighten up a small, dark space.

Though we often focus on the things that fill a room, wall and ceiling treatments form the setting for everything else and can make or break the design scheme.

Wall coverings

With the seemingly endless piles of sample books in most wallpaper stores, you may wonder how you'll ever find just the right paper. The best strategy is to have a clear idea of what your wallpaper should look like, where you'll hang it, and what material it should be. Most stores will let you take sample books home briefly; or, for a small charge, you may be able to buy a larger sample to keep as long as you like.

The most practical wallpapers, especially for do-it-yourselfers, have some vinyl content. Vinyl's strength makes these papers relatively easy to install; they're also easy to maintain.

Sturdy *fabric-backed vinyl* has a vinyl top layer and an undersurface of fiberglass or cheesecloth. *Vinyl-coated paper*, made of paper coated with a thin layer of vinyl, seems more like paper than vinyl and has a more sophisticated look. But whether they're inexpensive or costly, wall coverings made of *solid paper* without any vinyl all tend to tear easily.

Wallpapers and borders like those shown here add soft, traditional charm. But before you choose a paper, consider the territory: hard-use areas such as kids' rooms might require tougher, washable vinyl products.

WALLPAPER: LAURA ASHLEY INC.

However, they require an absolutely smooth wall surface and special installation, since they wrinkle easily.

The texture of a *flocked paper* resembles damask or cut velvet. Because flocks are hard to work with, it's best to have them professionally installed.

Fabric

Whether it's crisp chintz, informal canvas, or shimmering moiré, fabric makes walls come alive with color, pattern, and texture. Like no other wall covering, fabric lends softness and warmth to a room.

Home-decorating and uphol-stery fabrics are excellent choices for

Soundproofing Options

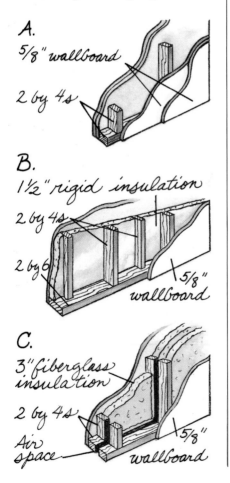

A.
5/8" wallboard

2 by 4s

B.
1½" rigid insulation

2 by 4s

2 by 6

5/8" wallboard

C.
3" fiberglass insulation

2 by 4s

Air space

5/8" wallboard

In the master suite of this Florida home, a white headboard and vivid linens play off the bold orange walls. Yellow in the adjacent dressing room and bath counters the bedroom's bright orange.

walls. Available in widths up to 60 inches, these fabrics are usually treated with a repellent that inhibits stains. In addition, they're printed with pattern overlaps at the sel-vages, making it easy to match the pattern at the seams.

Upholstering walls with fabric and batting takes more time than stapling or pasting fabric on them, but once you've finished, you'll see that the results are worth the effort. Polyester batting under the fabric cushions the walls, provides sound-proofing and insulation, conceals wall blemishes, and gives the fabric

a soft, luxurious appearance. Trim, usually double welt, is used to finish the edges.

With *stapled walls,* you stitch together panels of fabric in the same way as for upholstered walls, but you don't have to work over batting. If you want to simulate the look of upholstered walls and increase the insulating and sound-absorbing qualities of the wall, choose a quilted fabric.

Pasting fabric to walls is easy to do, but the result reveals any bumps, cracks, or other wall damage—so walls must first be perfectly smooth.

Also, colored walls must be given a coat of primer so light-colored fabric won't appear tinted.

Wood

The two main types of paneling are solid-board and sheet paneling.

Generally, solid boards have edges specially milled to overlap or interlock. Hardwood boards are milled from such species as oak, maple, birch, and mahogany. Common softwoods include cedar, pine, fir, and redwood.

Sheet paneling is a catchall term for wall paneling that comes in large, machine-made panels—most often 4 by 8 feet. The two main types are plywood and hardboard.

You can get just about any species of hardwood and most of the major softwoods laminated onto the surfaces of plywood panels. Hardboard paneling is usually less expensive, but it's also less durable and more subject to warping and moisture damage.

Paint

When it comes to good old paint, your basic choices are latex and alkyd. Latex is easy to work with, and you can clean up wet paint with soap and water. Alkyd paint (often called oil-base paint) provides high gloss and will adhere a little better than latex; however, alkyds are harder to apply and require cleanup with mineral spirits.

Flat, eggshell, and satin latex are standard sheens for bedroom walls, which don't demand the glossy washability of kitchen or bathroom surfaces. (Kids' rooms are the exception.) Flat paint is the norm for ceilings; shinier surfaces tend to magnify flaws and attract attention.

An excellent choice for cabinets and woodwork is quick-drying, interior/exterior alkyd enamel. It has a brilliant, tilelike finish that's extremely durable.

Spirited hues and a lively mix of patterns typify French country cottons. For continuity, the upholstered walls wear the same fabric as the window and bed canopy. Companion borders and prints complete the coordinated look.

So-called faux (literally, "false") finishes produce in paint the appearance of other patterns or textures. In one kind of treatment, many closely related pastels are built up in thin, translucent layers with brushwork, by stippling, or by daubing with a rag or sponge. Other faux finishes are bolder—using layers of textured paint and/or contrasting colors to mimic anything from traditional wallpaper to modern art.

WINDOWS & DOORS

So-called "openings"—windows, skylights, and doors—bring light, air, views, and access to your bedroom retreat. Here's a look at your choices.

Window options

At first glance, the windows in your neighborhood may all look different because of the variety of sizes and shapes. But it's likely that they all fall into one of eight basic categories.

Widely used in traditional homes, *double-hung units* (see drawing on page 86) have two sashes—an upper, or outside, sash that moves down and a lower, or inside, sash that moves up in grooves in the frame.

Casements are hinged on their sides like doors and are cranked or pushed open, usually outward, for maximum ventilation.

A *sliding window* is basically a double-hung turned on its side.

Modern double-hung replacement windows frame an ocean view; above them, in the peaked gable, floats a pentagon of fixed glass. Trim grilles snap off for easy cleaning.

Ganged skylights combine light-gathering efficiency with dramatic design potential. The bedroom at right has openable, electric-powered units with sun-control blinds.

PHOTO COURTESY OF VELUX-AMERICA, INC.

PHOTO COURTESY OF ANDERSEN WINDOWS, INC.

Pocket doors offer a clean, uncluttered solution to door-swing problems and clearance headaches. This door looks arched, but it's not: the rectangular fir door simply slides in an arched opening. It's the curved door rail that creates the illusion.

ARCHITECT: BREDTHAUER / CURRAN & ASSOCIATES

New sliding doors unite elegant styling and space-efficiency with energy-saving construction. These white wood sliders are teamed with matching fixed side panels, creating a bedroom window wall that also leads outdoors.

Windows & Skylights

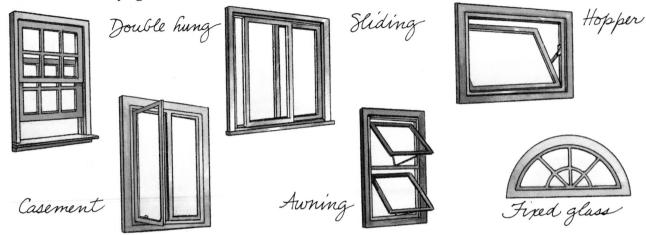

Double hung

Sliding

Hopper

Casement

Awning

Fixed glass

WINDOWS
& DOORS

However, it doesn't need the sometimes fickle balancing mechanisms used in double-hung designs. Sliders are available in larger sizes, too.

Awning windows are hinged at the top and open outward from the bottom. Often they're placed near larger fixed windows for ventilation; they also may be grouped vertically or side by side.

The opposite of awning windows, *hopper units* are hinged at the bottom and open inward from the top.

So-called *fixed windows* come in many standard versions, including rectangular, triangular, trapezoidal, semicircular, and elliptical. And if that's not enough, you can usually custom-order the exact shape and size your home requires.

Most *bays* have one or more straight center windows and angled side windows. *Bow windows* curve out, forming a narrow projection in the wall. Typically, you or your contractor adds the roof, support framing, and any flooring or seating.

Windows are available with frames made of wood, clad wood, aluminum, vinyl, steel, and fiberglass (a newcomer). Generally, aluminum windows are the least expensive, wood and clad wood the most costly.

Many of the greatest strides in window technology are taking place in glazing. Insulating glass is made of two or more panes of glass sealed together, with a space between the panes to trap air. Low-e (low-emissivity) glass usually consists of two sealed panes separated by an air space and a transparent coating.

Some manufacturers combine low-e glass with argon, a colorless, odorless gas pumped in and sealed between double panes to add extra insulation.

Skylight styles

You can pay as little as $100 for a fixed acrylic skylight, about $500 for a pivoting model that you crank open with a pole, or several thousand dollars for a motorized unit that automatically closes when a moisture sensor detects rain. The most energy-efficient designs feature double glazing and "thermal-break" construction.

Fixed skylights range in shape from square to circular; they may be flat, domed, or pyramidal in profile. So-called self-flashing models are generally for use on roofs with gentle slopes and shingled with thin mate-

Door Designs

Panel

Flush

French

Sliding

Bay Window

Bow Window

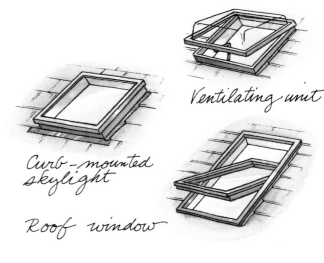

Curb-mounted skylight

Ventilating unit

Roof window

rials like wood, asphalt, or fiberglass. Curb-mounted skylights are used whenever the roof is covered with wood shakes, clay or concrete tiles, or slate, or whenever the slope is greater than 3 in 12.

Most skylight manufacturers offer at least one or two *ventilating models* that open to allow air in. You can operate them manually with the help of a pole or long cord or automatically using a power unit that works at the touch of a button.

Think of rotary *roof windows* as a cross between windows and opening skylights. They have sashes that rotate on pivots on each side of the frame, which permits easy cleaning and a range of ventilation angles. Unlike opening skylights, they are typically installed on sloping *walls*— such as in a finished attic, or wherever else you can reach them.

Door designs

You'll find a large, bewildering selection of doors at most lumberyards and home centers. Be on the lookout for the following types.

Interior doors. Though standard doors vary widely in both materials and appearance, they all come in two basic types: panel and flush.

Panel doors consist of solid vertical stiles and horizontal rails, with flat or raised panels in between. Panels may be replaced by one or more glass lights. Flush doors, on the other hand, are built from thin veneers attached to a solid or gridlike hollow core. Solid-core flush doors provide the best sound barriers. Whether it's panel or flush, the typical interior door is 1⅜ inches thick.

If space won't allow a swinging door, consider pocket, bifold, or accordion doors. A bifold door, which runs in a track, is hinged in the middle and folds out. A pocket door slides into a recess in the wall next to the opening. Accordion, or folding, doors allow you to temporarily close off one area from another.

Patio doors. French and sliding doors are traditional choices for bridging indoor and outdoor spaces.

French doors usually come in pairs, with an inactive door held stationary by slide bolts and an active door closing and locking against it. If you don't have room for a hinged door, you can opt for a slider. Factory-assembled units consist of two-door panels of tempered glass in a wood, vinyl, or aluminum frame.

Patio doors are usually 80 inches tall; the "standard" width is 6 feet, though smaller models are available from some manufacturers.

Single-light

Pocket

Bifold

Accordion

THE WORLD OF WINDOW TREATMENTS

Although some bedroom windows can stand alone, conditions such as decor, sun, or the need for privacy may call for special window treatments. Here's a look at five basic options: curtains, draperies, shades, shutters and screens, and blinds. For more information on both design and materials, see the *Sunset* book *Ideas For Great Window Treatments*.

Curtains

Once considered strictly casual, curtains have now earned a place in even the most elegant interiors. That's not to say that informal curtains are relics of the past; rather, the choices are now wonderfully varied, from short cafés to billowy floor-length panels, and from simple gathered headings to crisp-looking tabs.

By definition, curtains are either gathered on a rod or attached to a rod by tabs, rings, or ties. If curtains open and close, they're moved by hand.

If you lack the time, desire, or budget for a custom window treatment, ready-to-hang curtains or draperies may serve your purposes handsomely. They're sold in department stores, home-furnishing stores, specialty shops, and mail-order outlets.

Linings increase the life of the curtains, reduce noise, block light, and add insulation. Lined curtains have more body and hang better than unlined ones. They also look better because, in most cases, the hems don't show from the front.

Draperies

Draperies used to be staid and predictable: pleated panels hanging from hooks attached to narrow traverse rods. But not anymore. A wealth of trims, new choices in hardware and fabric, and imaginative applications of headings have enlivened this traditional window covering.

Sheer fabrics filter daylight and give some daytime privacy, but at night you may want something heavier. Casement fabrics are traditional choices; like sheers, they soften a window, but they generally give greater privacy at night. Medium-weight and heavy fabrics lend a formal, classic look and provide good insulation, light control, and nighttime privacy.

Lining your drapery fabric protects against fading, adds insulation, and makes the draperies look fuller and hang better. An interlining sandwiched between the drapery fabric and lining provides even more insulation.

Shades

From tailored roller and Roman styles to frothy Austrian and balloon creations, shades are as versatile in use as they are varied in style. They provide privacy, block light, and conserve energy.

Although shades that roll up or draw up in tidy or billowing folds are still very popular, innovative high-tech styles are making inroads in the market. New styles include pleated shades with an insulating honeycomb design and shades that roll up but have fabric slats that tilt like Venetian blinds to control light. You can also buy "double" shades, housing both blackout and diffusing layers.

Roman shades draw up into neat horizontal folds, Austrian shades into scalloped folds, and balloon shades into billows. All have rings on the back through which cords are strung.

Shutters & Screens

In some situations, hard-edged treatments such as shutters and screens lend elegance, simplicity, and architectural interest to a bedroom. When closed, solid-panel shutters block all light. Louvered shutters, lattice screens, and the more delicate Japanese shojis allow varying amounts of light to enter.

Traditional shutters have 1¼-inch louvers set in panels approximately 8 to 12 inches wide. Plantation shutters have wide louvers—most commonly 2½ to 4½ inches—set in panels roughly 15 to 36 inches wide. Wide louvers offer more ventilation and a clearer view than narrower ones.

Blinds

Although they differ in appearance, all blinds have slats that stack up or off the window's glazing and tilt for privacy and light control.

Venetian blinds, the original horizontal blinds, have 2-inch-wide slats held together by cotton tapes or nylon cords. Miniblinds, an updated, pared-down version of Venetian blinds, feature 1-inch metal or vinyl slats that tilt when you turn a wand. Miniblinds come in a wide range of colors and patterns.

Vertical blinds have all the advantages of horizontal blinds as well as the side-draw operation of draperies. Their wide slats can be made of PVC, fabric, wood, painted aluminum, or polycarbonate plastic; some slats have grooves for wallpaper or fabric strips to match or complement walls or furnishings.

Handsome window treatments needn't hide what's outside. French-pleated curtains (above) are held back by brass medallions to permit a full view. Soft-fold Roman shade (below) in gemstone-colored cotton print lifts to let sunlight enter. Louvered shutters (right) frame the view through patio doors and highlight windows behind a four-poster bed.

ARCHITECT: ROBERT H. WATERMAN/WATERMAN & SUN.
INTERIOR DESIGNER: ROBERT W. MILLER, ASID/FLEGEL'S

A SHOPPER'S GUIDE **89**

LOORING

Children's rooms require durable, skid-resistant floor coverings. But in a master bedroom, the only real requirement is comfort. Will it be carpeting, wood, resilient flooring, or tile? Let aesthetics and economics lead you to your decision. For help, visit flooring suppliers and home-improvement centers; most dealers are happy to provide samples.

Carpeting

Because of its low maintenance and inherent creature comfort, carpeting is a popular choice for bedrooms. Carpeting is commonly available in wool, acrylic, nylon, polypropylene, and polyester, as well as in combinations of these materials.

Half a dozen basic manufacturing processes are used to produce carpeting. Among the resulting styles are plush or velvet, level loop, sculptured pile, and shag. The best carpets are still loom-woven, though tufted carpet is more economical.

Wool is still considered tops in terms of wear and appearance, is simpler to clean than synthetics, and allows the greatest diversity in texture and design. The popular "Berber" style is one example of a nubby, loop-pile wool look that's hard to imitate in other materials.

Generally, man-made carpeting causes fewer allergies than do natural materials. Because of its durability, 100-percent nylon is a good choice for heavy-use areas or kids' rooms. Nylon carpeting is available in a wide range of colors and intensities. Most nylon carpets have a built-in static resistance. Spills wipe up more easily if the carpet is also treated with a stain repellent.

Sisal, a woven grass atop a backing, is popular and relatively inexpensive. However, sisal is not very practical for heavily used areas. Sisal/wool blends and 100-percent wool "sisal" are both tougher, easier-to-clean alternatives.

A low-pile or short-loop, densely woven carpet is best if it's going into a nursery or toddler's room (a deep shag might conceal small objects that a toddler could find and swallow). Plush carpets also hold a lot of dust, which is unhealthy for those with allergies. A medium color will show soiling less than a very light or dark color.

Floor choices include (clockwise from foreground) synthetic, sisal, and wool Berber carpeting; floating, strip, and parquet wood flooring; sheet and tile-form vinyl and textured-rubber resilients; tinted cork; and, in the small chips at center, a tough new composite fabricated from recycled materials.

Wood

A classic hardwood floor creates a warm decor, feels good underfoot, and can be refinished. Oak is most common, but many other species, including maple, birch, and pine, are also available.

The three basic types are narrow *strips* in random lengths; *planks* in various widths and random lengths; and wood *tiles*, laid in blocks or squares. Floating floor systems have several veneered strips atop each tongue-and-groove backing board. Wood flooring may be factory-finished or installed unfinished, to be sanded and finished in place.

You can clear-finish a wood floor with penetrating resin or polyurethane, stain it, paint it, pickle it, bleach it, stencil it, or use a combination of techniques. New water-base finishes are more user-friendly to apply than their oil-base relatives, resist yellowing, and seem as tough as traditional varnish or even tougher.

Resilients

If you think all resilient goods have a hard-times aura about them, think again: the selection of materials, colors, patterns, and textures now available is inspiring. And with a polyurethane finish, there is no need for waxing.

Generally made from solid vinyl or polyurethane, traditional resilients are flexible, moisture and stain resistant, easy to install, and simple to maintain. Sheets run up to 12 feet wide, eliminating seaming in small bedrooms; tiles are generally 12 inches square and can be mixed to form custom patterns or provide color accents as borders or banding.

Some vinyl still comes with a photographically applied pattern, but most is inlaid; the latter wears much better, though it is also more expensive.

Traditional linoleum is making a comeback, impregnated with natural materials like nut shells and fibers; nonskid varieties are available. High-tech designs often utilize imported rubber, sold in strips or squares; you can buy it plain, marbleized, or with raised patterns such as "steel plate" or dots—and in a variety of colors. Another popular look is cork, applied in strips atop a vinyl backing.

For a romantically old-fashioned look, an old strip floor was whitewashed with translucent paint, stenciled with floral and butterfly motifs in the field and checks and stripes around the edges, then sealed with a clear finish.

A multihued geometric rug forms a bold transition zone between the upholstered chair above it and the golden-oak strip flooring below it. Carpet retailers can often seam diverse edging and field components into one custom covering.

LIGHTING

Today's designers separate lighting into three categories: task, ambient, and accent. Task lighting illuminates a particular area where a visual activity—such as reading, bill-paying, or grappling with the VCR—takes place. Ambient, or general, lighting fills the undefined areas of a room with a soft level of light—enough, say, to shuffle to and from bed for a midnight snack. Accent, or mood, lighting, primarily decorative in its function, is used to highlight architectural features or art pieces, to set a mood, or to provide drama.

One of several lighting plans might meet your bedroom lighting needs; the "right" fixtures should match your design scheme, too. But before fixture shopping, take a tip from lighting pros: consider the source, or the bulb, first.

A look at bulbs & tubes

Light sources can be grouped according to the way they produce light. A collection of representative bulbs is shown at left.

Incandescent light. This light, the kind used most frequently in our homes, is produced by a tungsten thread that burns slowly inside a glass bulb. "A" bulbs are the old standbys; "R" and "PAR" bulbs produce a more controlled beam; silvered-bowl types diffuse light and cut glare. A number of decorative bulbs are also available.

Low-voltage incandescent lighting is especially useful for accent lighting. Operating on 12 or 24 volts, these lights require transformers (often built into the fixtures) to step down the voltage from standard 120-volt household circuits.

Fluorescent light. Fluorescent tubes are unrivaled for energy efficiency; they also last far longer than incandescent bulbs.

In the past, fluorescent tubes have been criticized for noise, flicker, and poor color rendition. Electronic ballasts and better fixture shielding against glare have remedied the first two problems; as for the last one, manufacturers have developed fluorescents in a wide spectrum of colors, from very warm (about 2,700 degrees Kelvin) to very cool (about 6,300 degrees Kelvin).

Here's a sampling of light sources and switches for bedroom use. Shown clockwise from upper left: fluorescent options, including U-shaped and globe retrofits for standard fixtures; frosted, clear, and nonglare incandescent bulbs; popular MR-16 and other halogen sources; and new dimmer designs.

These days, it's much simpler to blend fluorescent with tungsten or halogen sources than in the past. And you're no longer limited to big, clunky tubes. Compact fluorescent bulbs fit downlights and other compact fixtures and can be retrofitted to standard incandescent lamps with the use of an adapter.

Quartz halogen. These bright, white newcomers are excellent for task lighting, pinpoint accenting, and other dramatic accents. Halogen is usually low-voltage but may be standard line current. The popular MR-16 bulb creates the tightest beam; for a longer reach and wider coverage, choose a PAR bulb. There's an abundance of smaller bulb shapes and sizes that fit task lamps, pendants, and undercabinet strip lights.

Halogen has two disadvantages: high initial cost and its very high heat. Be sure to shop carefully; some fixtures on the market are not UL-approved.

What fixtures are best?

For bedrooms, you can choose among surface, recessed, movable, and adjustable fixtures. The key is combining them into an effective lighting scheme.

General room lighting. The most common, but hardly the most compelling, source of ambient bedroom lighting is a central ceiling fixture. But any time you step between the light source and something you're trying to see, you cast a shadow. When you reach into a drawer with your back to the fixture, you'll throw a shadow right over your blue, black, and brown socks—tough enough to tell apart in broad daylight.

A better plan is to use wall fixtures or place downlights or shielded uplights on the perimeter of the ceiling. Small track lights are also useful for both overall and mood effects.

Graceful wall sconces (below) supplement natural light during the day when necessary and at night give ambient and accent lighting.

Small, discreet, and directional are the bywords of modern lighting. A recessed downlight (top) rotates to supply light where it is needed; trim track fixtures (bottom) move along tracks and pivot, providing accurate aim.

Adjustable lamps put task light where you want it and—as this one shows—don't have to be boring. This swing-arm model is ideal for reading, either by a bed or a comfortable chair.

Here's custom lighting for a custom headboard. Fluorescent tubes behind an overhead soffit supplement small overhead downlights, baffled for bedtime reading. All controls are housed in the headboard.

ARCHITECT: MORIMOTO ARCHITECTS

A LOOK AT ELECTRONICS

As more and more homeowners are discovering, the master bedroom makes a great hub for activities such as watching videos and listening to music. Today's multifaceted bedroom is also a natural spot for home computing and networking tasks. If you're remodeling, why not consider these needs, too?

Home Theater Basics

Maybe you'd prefer to gather in the living room or den, but if you're planning an up-to-date audio-visual center for your bedroom, you'll have some logistics to work out.

For starters, you'll need a monitor, 35 inches or larger. It can be either a rear-projection unit or a classic silver screen, even one that retracts from the ceiling when needed.

Next, you'll want a hi-fi VCR or laser disc player. True surround-sound requires at least three amplifiers and five strategically placed speakers (plus optional subwoofer for a booming, theater-like bass). An additional component, the signal decoder, routes sound to the appropriate speakers. Though most designers choose separates, you can also find a number of integrated components that house amplifiers, preamp controls, and decoder in one case.

Where do you put it all? Either in custom or modular cabinetry or inside the wall, utilizing space borrowed from an adjacent closet or room. There are two basic rules for housing electronic gear: you must allow air circulation, and you must be able to get at component backs when connecting and servicing them. A number of compact speakers are specially designed for wall installation.

The Smart Bedroom

It's coming—the day when your built-in house system not only controls light and temperature automatically but links you directly to outside communication systems via computer chip and modem.

As we spend more time in our master suites and private retreats, it also makes sense to make this area the nighttime command center for house-wide operations. Bedside control panels not only allow you to monitor and access both interior and exterior lights but can handle security sensors, alarms, and an intercom, too.

It's expected that the "smart" house will eventually be wired via a central raceway or house "core." So if you're planning an extensive remodel, why not discuss this addition with your architect or designer? Later, you could route specific cables and connectors.

If you install dimmer controls, your overall lighting can also be used for mood lighting. The bright "get-dressed-and-get-out-the-door" light can be subdued to a more reposeful level by a twist of a knob.

Bedside task lighting. A light source you can reach from bed is a necessity. As long as switches are within arm's reach, the fixture can be recessed in the ceiling, attached to the wall next to or behind the bed, placed on an adjacent table, or built into the headboard or frame.

Adjustable lamps are, in many people's opinion, the best for in-bed reading. Whether you sit bolt upright turning pages as fast as you can to find out "whodunit" or recline to court sleep with a volume of poetry, an adjustable lamp can turn and tilt with you. And with an adjustable light, you can read into the late hours without disturbing a partner.

If you prefer a nonadjustable lamp with a shade, place it so the lower edge of the shade is at eye level while you're in an angle of repose. The lamp should ideally be about 22 inches away from your bed. Adjustable or not, reading light should be directed onto the page from the side, not from overhead.

Mood lighting. You can also mingle light and shadow to create dramatic accents or special effects. Try focusing a wall washer or monospot on a favorite plant. Picture lights can be installed on the wall or on the artwork's frame. Objects on a shelf can be illuminated by low-voltage downlights or strip lights tucked behind valances. Uplights might graze a graceful ficus or add a little gentle mystery to an open corner; or use a decorative screen and shine light behind it. As with overall lighting, the fastest and easiest way to adjust your room's mood lighting is with dimmers.

Bedroom electronics often call for imaginative installations. The master bedroom at left houses its projector unit at the foot of the bed; audio components and theater amplifiers sit behind a built-in storage unit's drawer fronts and doors. Above, a bedside control panel with switches for lighting, security, and audio systems is arranged for nighttime access.

INDEX

Boldface numbers refer to photographs

Photographers: